A
Cast of Friends

A
Cast of Friends

Bill Hanna

with Tom Ito

TAYLOR PUBLISHING COMPANY
DALLAS, TEXAS

To Violet

Copyright © 1996 William Hanna and Tom Ito

All rights reserved.

No part of this may be reproduced in any form or by any means—including photocopies or electronic media—without written permission from the publisher.

Published by
Taylor Publishing Company
1550 West Mockingbird Lane
Dallas, Texas 75235

All Hanna-Barbera characters courtesy and © Hanna-Barbera Productions, Inc.
Tom and Jerry courtesy and © Turner Entertainment Co.

Designed by Timmons Willgren Design

Frontispiece: Joe Barbera and I showing Fred Quimby a Tom and Jerry story at MGM in 1946.

Library of Congress Cataloging-in-Publication Data

Hanna, William, 1910-
    A cast of friends / Bill Hanna with Tom Ito ; foreword by Joe Barbera.
      p. cm.
    Includes index.
    ISBN 0-87833-916-7
    1. Hanna, William, 1910-   . 2. Animators—United States-
-Biography. I. Ito, Tom. II. Title.
    NC1766.U52H342 1996
    741.5'8'092—dc20
    [B]
                                          95-39322
                                          CIP

Printed in the United States of America
10 9 8 7 6 5 4 3 2 1

Acknowledgments

I n four score and some odd years, I've been blessed by being able to share a wonderful life with a treasury of family and friends.

I wish to express my deepest gratitude to my wife, Violet, who has been the inspiration for every one of my aspirations in life.

I also wish to thank my son, David, and my daughter, Bonnie, for all of the loving support and encouragement they have shown in this endeavor. Special thanks as well to my grandchildren: Laurie Hanna, Molly Hanna, William Hanna, John Hanna, David Williams, Philip Williams, and Emily Williams.

A creative partnership that endures is in itself nothing less than miraculous. I offer a special salute to my lifelong creative partner, Joe Barbera, who has with me lived so much of the story within these pages.

Over the years, many friends and colleagues have shared the adventures and misadventures of my life. Heartfelt thanks to the following people who have kindly relived many of the wonderful memories that nourished this book: Neil Balnaves, Jayne Barbera, Shari Belafonte, Tony Benedict, Hoyt Curtin, Pat Foley, Nancy Grimaldi, Barbara Krueger, Alison Leopold, Margaret Loesch, Don Lusk, Ray Patterson, Nelda Ridley, Maggie Roberts, Paul Sabella, Art Scott, Fred Seibert, Jerry Smith, the late Irven Spence, Iwao Takamoto, Carl Urbano, James Wang, Richard Wilson, and Star Wirth.

Finally, a handshake in friendship and appreciation to my friend and co-author, Tom Ito, my assistant, Ginger Robertson, and our editor, Holly McGuire. We are all veterans now and fellow conjurers.

Contents

Foreword
by Joe Barbera

Long before the debut of such signature Hanna-Barbera characters as Yogi Bear and Fred Flintstone, Bill Hanna and I tossed a coin to decide which of our names would come first in the logo of our partnership. Bill won the toss, but I never minded a bit. As far as we were both concerned, the partnership of Hanna-Barbera was a winning combination from either end.

I first met Bill Hanna in 1937. The two of us were the rookies among a group of veteran animators, artists, and writers who had been recruited by Metro-Goldwyn-Mayer to participate in the creation of a cartoon studio.

Bill and I ended up sitting opposite each other in the same office, and it was then that we both sensed we would make a good team. Just a few months later, we created and produced that irrepressible cat-and-mouse team Tom and Jerry, and the die was cast.

Bill Hanna and I continued to happily produce Tom and Jerry cartoons for nearly two decades, until one fateful day it all ended. MGM abruptly closed its cartoon studio and nearly two hundred people, including Bill and me, were out of a job.

That was when Bill and I decided to flip a coin and bet on ourselves. We formed our own company, Hanna-Barbera Productions, and charted a course of producing cartoons for what was then virtually a new and untapped market, television.

That was back in 1957, and today Bill and I are as in love with the business of making cartoons as ever. Shakespeare once asked, "What's in a name?" For Bill Hanna and myself, the name of Hanna-Barbera inaugurated a lifelong creative alliance that I will always cherish.

Preface

By Stone Age standards, Fred Flintstone was a blue-collar kind of a guy. As part of the signature opening for *The Flintstones* television series, a huge steam whistle would blow, signaling quitting time at the Bedrock quarry. Fred would give out an exuberant "Yabba-Dabba-Doo!," expressing his joy at the day's work being over, and race home to Wilma. Fred Flintstone has always been my personal favorite of all the Hanna-Barbera cartoon characters. In fact, Fred and I have a great deal in common. We have both been rather explosive at times in temperament, and occasionally even a little belligerent. But Fred, as I like to believe I am, was also basically good-hearted, down to earth, and fiercely loyal to his friends.

There is one point, however, on which we sharply differed. Fred was strictly a nine-to-five fellow. He punched a time clock and when that whistle blew, he exited the job as fast as his footmobile could carry him. For the greater part of my own life, work here at our "cartoon quarry" has been my natural habitat. Chances are, if a whistle ever blew at the studio, I would never have heard it.

I have worked at the same job as a producer of animation since 1930, and I love the business today as much as ever. After sixty years, I still get up at six o'clock in the morning, take a short walk around the neighborhood, and have breakfast with my wife, Violet. By nine, I am in my office at the studio where I put in a full workday among coworkers, many of whom are longtime friends and as close to me as family.

That agenda provides the basic core of my life today, although there have been intense changes during the six-decade era of my professional life. I have been fortunate in the fact that I have enjoyed a career rich with challenges, rewards, and, above all, friendships which have provided the real substance of my life's experiences.

I sometimes like to joke with associates that "cartoons have always been a moving experience for me." There is actually more truth than poetry in that remark. Producing animation entertainment with my longtime partner, Joe Barbera, along with the corps of talented and industrious artists, animators, technicians, and other folks with whom we worked, has been an emotional journey filled with both joy and disappointment.

Over the years a lot of labels have been attached to the team of Hanna-Barbera and our creations. I have heard Joe and me touted as "pioneers in the field of animation" and many of our popular cartoon personalities such as Yogi Bear and Fred Flintstone referred to as "classic Hanna-Barbera characters." All I know is that both Joe and I have been at this business a very long time, and we've been lucky enough to have many of the cartoon shows we've produced become enduring and enjoyable entertainment for our audiences.

When you're at a job as long as I've been, I guess you're bound to eventually be labeled a pioneer or maybe a relic of some sort. Admittedly, I've seen a lot of changes in the animation industry, yet one thing remains constant. The human relationships and deep friendships I have enjoyed with countless coworkers throughout the storyboards of my life have been my greatest joy. From titles to credits, the real magic of my memories is created by a cast of friends.

Bill Hanna

Chapter One

Rhymes and Reasons

I was born in Melrose, New Mexico on July 14, 1910. I suppose anything that occurred in 1910 would today be considered an historical event. There were a number of things other than my birthday, however, going on that year that I feel really qualify as history. In 1910, William Howard Taft was President of the United States. Henry Ford aggressively embarked on a revolutionary production concept called the assembly line and declared that he would create a car for every man in the country.

In addition, there were two other events of particular personal interest to me that occurred that year. First, a wonderful new organization called the Boy Scouts of America was chartered in Washington, D.C. At the same time, a newspaperman by the name of Winsor McCay was intently involved in the animation of an engaging cartoon strip called *Little Nemo* that would debut as a short cartoon the following year. Both of these events would have great significance in my life a little later on.

In my family, the womenfolk outnumbered the menfolk, but there was no war between the sexes. My father was named William John Hanna and my mother's maiden name was Avice Joyce Denby. I was the third of seven children—and the only son. My six sisters were Lucille, Connie, Norma, Marion, Evelyn, and Jessilee. We formed a very close family, and I cannot recall any sibling rivalry between any of us kids at all.

Still, as was commonly quoted in those days, "Boys will be boys, and girls will be girls." Rather than referring to me as his son, Dad usually preferred to call me "Brother," and I suspect that this was done partially out of some sort of male bonding instinct to provide me with a comrade in a brood where my gender was so obviously in the minority.

I shared a strong fellowship with my dad. He was chief companion, cohort, and coworker. Employed as a superintendent for the Thomas Haverty Company, Dad oversaw the construction and development of water and sewer systems throughout extensive western regions of the country. Some of my earliest and happiest boyhood memories are of accompanying him to some of the work camps where he ran the crews.

When I was about three years old, my father moved the family from New Mexico to Baker, Oregon, where he was assigned to work on the construction of the Balm Creek Dam. It was a beautiful work site set in the midst of lush forests and grassy meadowlands. I can remember Dad taking me along with him to this camp, where he supervised the crew. These were generally overnight excursions, and, although they were just part of the job for my father, they seemed to me at the time to be the height of robust adventure.

For some reason, my memories of that woodland camp have remained surprisingly vivid over the eight intervening decades of my life. I can recall a clear, cold water stream swarming with trout. On one occasion, some of the crewmen dammed up one side of the stream to form a kind of stock pond of trout, and you could literally reach in and grab the fish for your supper.

Because of my extreme youth, I was excused from any camp duties other than maybe being an unofficial observer. I remember seeing a lot of booted feet and legs in rough dungarees moving around in industrious activity under my father's sure-handed and disciplined supervision. Left to my own devices, I did a lot of exploring. Since I was a lot closer to the ground than everybody else, I discovered an assortment of earthly treasures ranging from rocks and tree bark to clusters of pine cones.

At mealtimes, Dad saw to it that I was provided with special accommodations. A square five-gallon can was set on one end to provide me with a table and I was given a little sawed-off log about eight or ten inches high as a chair. The cook would bring over a plate laden with fried fish, and I can remember sitting at my little five-gallon oil can and eating the most delicious trout I ever enjoyed in my life.

When kids tire of collecting things, they often turn to mischief. I was no exception. Adjacent to our house in Baker was a chicken house about forty feet long with little glass windows about a foot square in size. One day I got the bright idea of throwing a rock at one of the windows to test my aim. To my surprise the rock cracked the glass, sending out a beautiful spiral pattern in all directions. I told my older sister, Lucille, about this phenomenon, and together we spent the afternoon throwing rocks and cracking every damn window in that place trying to make pretty designs. Sometimes a rock would go clear through and sometimes the rock wouldn't hit the glass hard enough, but we kept at it. By the end of the day we had produced these sparkling designs in most of the chicken house windows.

I don't remember either of us catching any hell from Dad for that artistic experiment or for many other mischievous things that we did. As a matter of fact, I can only recall getting spanked by my father once or twice, and even then he was very reluctant to do it. The one occasion I remember being punished occurred when I was in grammar school. A place called Leeks Lake, located several blocks away from home, had donkeys and horses that could be rented out for riding to kids at about ten cents an hour. One day after school I headed for the lake without first letting my folks know where I was going. I was gone for several hours, thoroughly enjoying myself with the horses and donkeys. When I finally got home, I found Mother tight-lipped with anger. Only she didn't remain tight-lipped for very long. In no uncertain words, she insisted to my father that he deliver a spanking to me for thoughtlessly worrying the family.

Father looked at Mother and then he looked at me. I had placed him in a tough dilemma and although it didn't seem like it to me at the time, the prospect of giving me the strap must have hurt him more than it hurt me. Reluctantly, he led me to the bedroom and removed his belt. "Bend over," he told me almost apologetically. It seemed as if I was not going to be in shape to get in a donkey's saddle, or for that matter any kind of seat, for some time.

I complied in trembling obedience. "Now, Brother," said my dad in a low tone, "I want you to cry loud enough so that your mother can hear so that she'll be convinced you're getting a real spanking."

When I looked at that inch-and-a-half-wide belt, I thought that "crying loud enough" was going to be the least of my problems. A moment later the belt came down grazing my bottom and smacking more into the chair than on me. Relief flooded over me, but I kept my presence of mind and took my cue. I let loose with a loud wail that made Dad cringe even though he really hadn't hurt me. A few minutes later, I returned to the family fold with a look of proper chastisement. From then on I always asked permission before I visited the donkeys.

I do not want to mislead anyone into believing that Mother was the tyrant of the family. She was not. Like many women at that time, Mother was the often unsung heroine of the clan, descended from a formidable pioneer strain of females, who were the real hewers of wood and carriers of water in the country. (Her father, my grandfather, T.B.S. Denby, was a circuit judge in the then-territory of New Mexico.) Mother was a tenderhearted woman, but she was also strong-willed, a devout Christian, and firmly resolved that her children would grow up as God-fearing, kindly, industrious people. She shouldered much of the burden and responsibility of raising seven children, for Dad's construction work kept him away from home a great deal of time.

Mother was a woman with true grit, and we children were often witness to her mettle. In her own way she could be as generous as Dad with folks, but she would not allow any of her family to be trespassed upon. There was one particular occasion I remember when Mother made it clearly evident that those boundaries had been crossed. The house we lived in at Baker stood on about ten acres of land and included our celebrated chicken house as well as a section of ground where Dad grew corn.

One day while our father was away on a job, a woman from a nearby Gypsy camp boldly ventured into our chicken house and without permission helped herself to as many eggs as she could carry in her apron. As she emerged from the henhouse, the woman was confronted by a resolute Avice Denby Hanna. Mother sternly reclaimed her property before dismissing the woman, who went home with very few eggs.

A very pious woman, Mother insisted that her children attend church regularly. Dad was inclined to attend church rather irregularly, a practice sometimes happily emulated by his only son, much to Mother's dismay. Religion was never a thundering issue in our family. Devout as Mother was, she was never dogmatic in the religious training of her children, and as kids I think we all instinctively followed the strong examples of morality and common sense set by both our parents as they lived their lives.

It saddens me sometimes to see how complex many contemporary family relationships seem to have become. Admittedly, my childhood was spent in a simpler time. The "basics" of life, including such fundamental perspectives as respecting the dignity of work, overlooking other people's shortcomings, and extending human kindness, may have been given to us in plain wrapping by our folks, but they offered a substance and comfort of health and happiness. There were few lectures, no silent recriminations for past misdeeds, no lingering resentments, and as far as I can recall, no favoritism shown by either of our parents toward any of us kids.

That is not to say that we didn't have our share of squabbles and scraps. After all, we are talking about a red-blooded, Irish-American family. But despite differences and individual concerns, we were all ultimately counseled by that homespun ethic that was once embroidered into countless needlepoint samplers across the country: "Do Unto Others As You Would Have Others Do Unto You."

When I was about five, Dad moved the family to Logan, Utah, where he'd obtained work supervising the construction of a railroad station. Mother promptly saw to it that all of us children were installed in the local school, and I began my formal education in the first grade. The old cliché preached by generations of parents to their children about having to walk a mile to school in the snow in their youth has some bearing in my case. My sisters and I did begin classes during a snowy winter in Logan. Mother bundled us up and sent us off, but it generally wasn't into the teeth of a blizzard, and the schoolhouse was only a few blocks away.

The paved road that led to school was covered with snow. Rather than trudging through the drifts, however, a lot of us kids gleefully made other arrangements. Very often horse-drawn sleighs with runners about four inches wide would drive down the street, and many of us would jump onto the runners and hitch a ride to school holding onto the side of the wagon. A few minutes later we would all tramp into the classroom with wet, cold feet; I can remember our schoolteacher taking off our shoes and rubbing our feet with her hands to get them warm again.

On the whole, we were all a pretty rambunctious bunch of kids. The grandparents and great-grandparents who to new generations now appear so blue-veined, paper-skinned and eternally apprehensive of breaking a hip were, once upon a time, shrieking young daredevils apparently invulnerable to the elements of rain, snow, sleet and the perils of reckless impetuosity.

I could be as heedless as any of my cohorts. On one occasion, sometime during our second year living in Logan, I spotted a bird's nest high up in the branches of a tree that stood in our front yard. Obeying all my natural impulses, I began climbing up the branches toward the nest, leaving the ground far below. Just before I got to the nest, I came upon a big spider who suddenly appeared on his web right in front of me. Panicked, I let go of the branches and fell to the ground and broke my arm.

That was in 1917. In the same year, Dad secured his position as a supervisor with the Thomas Haverty Company, and we made the move to California and settled in San Pedro for about two years. My arm was still in a sling as we boarded the train to California. During the next few years, we changed residences frequently, moving from San Pedro to a rented cottage on 69th Street in Los Angeles and eventually in 1919 to a small house at 9523 Anzac Avenue in Watts, California.

I made friends easily wherever we lived, but it was while we were living in Watts that I actually developed a small circle of chums with whom I would remain acquainted for many years. One of these boys was a fellow by the name of G.D. Atkinson. He was an ingenious kind of a guy who helped me build a crystal set; it was the only kind of radio our family ever owned when I was a boy. The device seemed a genuine technical marvel to me at the time, and featured an impressive circuitry of wires and crystals contained in a tubelike shell. Suddenly, evenings promised a special new adventure. At nights I would go to bed holding that little thing to my ear, and in the darkness the wonderful music of a band playing at the Coconut Grove would fill my room.

G.D. Atkinson and I had two other pals about our age by the name of Bill Tweedy and Jack Ogden. One day these two fellows told us about an organization they'd heard about called the Boy Scouts that offered an appealing program of outdoor activities and instruction in lifesaving skills. For a bunch of twelve-year-old-boys, this outfit sounded irresistibly adventurous.

With my parents' encouragement, we contacted a man named Ed Baxter, who was the scoutmaster of Troop 2 of the Watts District, and signed up to be Boy Scouts. It was that simple. There wasn't a lot of formality or ceremony in becoming a scout in those days. Although we were required to buy our own uniforms, the cost was not that great. I had a newspaper route at that time and used my earnings to buy the simple khaki outfit that I donned with great pride.

With the enlistment of Bill Tweedy, Jack Ogden, and myself, the ranks of Troop 2 swelled to an impressive legion of twelve. Ed Baxter proved to be an enthusiastic scoutmaster, and I remember several of us piling into his car and going down to Redondo Beach for a regular part of our scouting activities. For five or ten cents, we would be admitted to the swimming pool there, where we learned to swim and were trained in lifesaving skills.

The most adventurous activities involved camping. Many of these excursions merely involved the troop going to the wash of a nearby riverbed in Watts, but I can remember one special trip where we all boarded a streetcar known in those days as the "Red Car" which carried us into Hollywood. The streetcar's route ended at the bottom of a little narrow dirt road known as Cahuenga Pass. There we disembarked and hiked up the pass to a Boy Scout camp in the Hollywood Hills, where we spent the weekend.

This was back in 1922. Despite its growing reputation as a primary motion picture center, Hollywood remained in great part a rustic community. The surrounding hills were still vacant grasslands, spotted with occasional scrub oak and sagebrush. Even at that time, however, much of this was rapidly changing and by the early 1920s, there were twenty motion picture studios in the Hollywood vicinity with each one vying for dominion in the film business.

Although the actual geography of Hollywood itself is undistinguished, vivid promoters like Sid Graumann were setting about to change all that by constructing such colossal manmade landmarks as theatres resembling exotic Chinese and Egyptian temples. The grassy ravines above Hollywood would be cleared and terraced, with mansions built that would transform the Hollywood Hills into a kind of terra-cotta Olympus.

Cahuenga Pass was fated to be widened, paved, and re-christened Cahuenga Boulevard. In the days of the Red Car and Troop 2's camping trek, however, it was still a rugged dirt trail of adventure for a squad of twelve-year-olds. The Pass challenged us with a fairly steep hike and as we trudged along with our sleeping bags, I hadn't the slightest inkling that about a half-mile beyond our trail lay a tract of land that would, thirty-five years later, become the site of our present animation studio.

Underlying all of the scouting activities is a fundamental set of principles that are set forth in a special creed known as the Scout Law. The universally known Boy Scout motto, "Be Prepared," was the essential theme of the organization regarding the life lessons it provided to boys. Preparation extended beyond merely insuring that we had our canteens and pocketknives available for camping trips. What the Boy Scouts endeavored to teach us were many of the character lessons regarding personal honor and service to others that prepared us to live sound, healthy, and constructive lives.

The ultimate goal most scouts endeavor to achieve through the process of promotions and earning merit badges, of course, is to be made an Eagle Scout. G.D. Atkinson, Bill Tweedy, myself, and others all became Eagle Scouts, and the pride of that award, like our friendships, has lasted throughout our lives. For over six decades many of the original members of Boy Scout Troop 2 of the Watts District continued to meet every year for a reunion, and I have attended nearly every gathering. Time and death have thinned the ranks of this boyhood battalion until only about six of us remain, but the memories of those days when we all pledged and endeavored to "help others at all times, to keep ourselves physically strong, mentally alert, and morally straight" have never diminished.

My friendships with schoolmates in no way ever lessened the strong comradeship with Dad. Throughout my boyhood, I spent many days working alongside him and his crew, first as a water boy, and later as a regular laborer on many of his construction assignments. Dad held a deep affection for his employees and his relationship with these people extended to a bond of family-like closeness. His innate modesty and broad sense of humanity seemed to touch everyone with whom he worked, and I can remember many of his workers bringing tubs of homemade tamales and jugs of red wine to our house out of their love and respect for my father.

Dad's easygoing and democratic nature encouraged an early sense of independence within me. I grew accustomed from a very young age to finding a job, learning and respecting manual labor, and making my own money. For ten cents I could go to one of the local theatres in town and enjoy a motion picture—and maybe a bag of popcorn. All of the motion pictures were silent in those days, but by God the screen really seemed to be silver, and film stars like Charlie Chaplin, Douglas Fairbanks, and Mary Pickford loomed larger than life. One of the major attractions of these films for me was the presentation of animated cartoon shorts preceding the movie.

I grew particularly fond of the funny antics of a Chaplinesque black cat named Felix whose idiosyncratic expressions and movements gave him a personality as unique as any of the live-action characters who followed. Seeing Felix the Cat was probably my first exposure to what would later popularly become known in the animation industry as "personality animation" and it made moviegoing a real event for me.

By my sophomore year in high school, I had saved up enough to buy my own car. I got a job working for an enterprising man named Dougherty who owned a restaurant that provided food services for several local schools, including my own high school in Compton. Among my principal tasks was that of making gallons of orange juice from a mountain of sliced citrus. I developed a kind of system where I could grab oranges with either my right or left hand, twist the fruit on the metal cone with its little moat tray to catch the juice, pour the orange juice through a strainer into a five-gallon crock, and reach for the next orange in an unbroken automatic rhythm.

It was an unglamorous and sticky job, but one of the principal attractions of working in that kitchen at the time was the owner's pretty daughter, Helen Dougherty, who became my high school sweetheart. Since I had six sisters, I wasn't particularly shy around girls. Surrounded by women in my family, I was constantly exposed to their inherent cultural appreciation of fine arts and refined behavior, and that eased a lot of my awkwardness in adolescent romance.

There were enough women in our family to form a proper sewing circle, but following the way of their talents, and being their own women, Mother and two of my sisters allied into more of a kind of literary-art circle. Mother loved to write and although she was never published, our family mementos include many beautiful poems and essays by her, primarily of a religious or spiritual nature, that reveal a sensitive and idealistic spirit.

Mother's writing, like everything else she did in life, was for her family. Although none of her compositions were ever published, they have remained for her children a loving legacy of that devotion.

In writing this memoir, I recently came across several large scrapbooks containing many of Mother's written works. Included was the following short poem recorded in faded ink in Avice Hanna's meticulous penmanship:

> To My Children
> To you whom I have loved so much
> I leave no houses land or gold
> For moth and dust corrupteth such
> And thieves break through to hold

Deep in my heart I've kept for you
The purple dusk of twilight hours
Stars from God's jewel case of blue
The perfume of bright summer flowers

I've kept for each a golden dream
Untarnished through the years
A faith as bright as sunlight's gleam
And a portion of sorrow and tears

I leave you a part of God's blue skies
A mother's love unfaltering true
The memory of soft lullabies
That once I crooned to you

I leave you sunny summer days
And woodland paths that we have trod
Best loved heritage to keep always
A child-like faith in God

Avice Joyce Hanna
July 1933

Mother's literary aspirations were emulated by my younger sister, Norma, who did go on to publish several essays and articles in numerous religious publications and who today still continues to write.

As children, we were all encouraged to follow our own interests and develop whatever talents we felt God had given us. My older sister, Lucille, elected to take piano lessons and proved to be a gifted musician. At the ripe old age of sixteen, I figured there had to be an artistic niche for me there somewhere. I decided to follow Lucille's example and took piano lessons. I soon concluded that my aesthetic flair, if I possessed one, was not to be found at an upright, and decided to seek my muse elsewhere.

The combined artistic endeavors of Mother and my sisters, however, did produce a singular impression on me. They imparted to me a great appreciation of rhythm, timing, and imagery. As mediums of expression, music and literature have often been the parents that conceived new art forms which, like children, bore resemblances to both parents, yet emerged with their own distinct individual personalities.

Admittedly, such realizations were beyond my ponderings as a child, but Lucille's piano playing along with Norma's and Mother's literary expressions provoked a kind of early restlessness within me. They had found individual identities through the happy discovery of an aptitude for a distinct art form. Maybe there was something yet unrevealed out there for me as well.

I fell into the practice of making up little verses and four-line poems and writing them down on paper. They were generally whimsical little things about cats and mice, boys and girls, good feelings and hope. I would make the verses up in my head by flirting with the way different words sounded and arranging them together to form a rhyme. It began as a game more than anything else, but composing these verses became a habit that has lasted a very long lifetime. To this day I still write occasional poems to celebrate a family birthday or maybe the Christmas season.

Some of my boyhood writings have managed to survive to see the light of the latter century. I recently came across a few of these poems packed in a film box stored in our garage. Included was this little rhyme composed for my younger sister, Evelyn, and is pretty typical of the kinds of things I was doing at the time.

> I have a brand new sister
> I haven't held her yet
> Each time I start to pick her up
> Her diaper's wringing wet

My interest in verse and music began in adolescence and has remained with me throughout my life. Growing up, I took both piano and saxophone lessons, and I later studied piano composition. None of these activities, however, stimulated me enough to consider seriously a career in either music or writing. During high school I favored studies in mathematics and journalism and was active in sports, but a clear vision of a life's profession still eluded me.

By the time I graduated from Compton High School in 1928, I had managed to make a number of decisions regarding my future, but they were all choices regarding what I distinctly knew *I did not want to do* with my life. First of all, I pretty much knew that I did not want to follow my father's profession of construction supervisor. I had spent a great part of my boyhood working with Dad on various jobs and had enjoyed the experiences, but the prospect of building a career in such work did not appeal to me. In addition, I knew that I was not cut out to be a musician or a twentieth-century Walt Whitman. Music and verse were always more diversions than serious occupations for me, and I had no intention nor could I afford to indulge living my life merely as a dilettante.

My parents, particularly Mother, had always wanted their children to attend college. Following graduation from high school, I entered Compton Junior College and began my studies there as a journalism major. That was in 1929. In that same year, the Great Depression plunged the entire country into economic disaster. Times were hard and I dropped out of college in order to try and find a job.

Suddenly all of my inconclusive speculation on how I was to build a future seemed irrelevant to the harsh reality of the times. The Depression had obliterated the hopes, dreams, and even the very lives of countless people who, like myself, probably never dreamed that such desperation could grip this country. Now all that seemed to matter was to get a job, any kind of job at all, and to hold on to it as long as possible.

By this time, my father had retired from his position with the Thomas Haverty Company and none of us were working. Fortunately, a contractor named C.L. Peck, who had once worked for my father as a foreman, contacted Dad and told him of a possible job in the construction of Pantages Theatre in Hollywood. Dad applied for and received a job as a crew supervisor and the family moved to a small rented house in Hollywood.

He also managed to get me a job with the same company working with the structural engineers on the theatre's construction, a job which earned me a paycheck of twenty dollars a week. The job called for me to assist the surveyors by carrying and holding the measuring rods, and often required me to walk across scaffolding spanning steel beams several stories off the ground. On one occasion I lost my footing and fell one story to the floor below and broke my arm. That mishap put me in the hospital, and while I was waiting for the fracture to mend, I did some serious thinking. "Bill," I reasoned to myself. "There might be a lesson in this for you." It was about that time that I decided that I would have to figure out a way of making a living for myself using my head rather than relying on sheer physical labor for employment.

Construction of the Pantages Theatre was completed in about six months and I was once again unemployed. Dad felt that he was getting too old to continue the rigorous work of a construction supervisor and returned to retirement. I had been lucky enough to hang onto my 1925 Ford Coupe, which I had bought from the earnings of previous odd jobs—now so preciously scarce. Every day I would make a circuit through downtown Hollywood, stopping at various places to inquire about work. And every day it was the same story. Heads shaking, apologies, nothing, nothing, nothing. I would always finish up the day at a service station owned by the Muller Brothers on Sunset Boulevard in the heart of Hollywood.

Sam Muller was a kindly man who had watched me forlornly make my rounds looking for work for some time. One afternoon as I pulled into the lot of his station and despondently watched them pump gasoline, he took pity on me and walked over to where I stood. "Bill," he said, "I've watched you come in here every day for two weeks now after looking for a job and coming back empty-handed. If you come back here tomorrow without a job, I'll give you work at the station washing cars."

That was the brightest ray of hope I'd seen in a long and dismal period. The next day, after another fruitless search for work, I returned to Muller Brothers, where, true to their word, they gave me a job that I took with heartfelt gratitude. I worked for about a week there washing cars, thankful for every second of employment and praying for the continued blessing of work.

One evening I got involved in a conversation with a fellow by the name of Jack Stevens who was dating my sister Marion. Jack worked for a company owned by Leon Schlesinger called Pacific Art & Title that produced titles and artwork for Warner Bros. Studio. Jack informed me that Schlesinger had contracted with two young artists, Hugh Harman and Rudolph Ising, to produce animated cartoons which Schlesinger was selling to Warner Bros. Harman and Ising had recently formed their own animation studio and were producing animated cartoons called "Looney Tunes" and "Merrie Melodies" for Schlesinger. Jack had learned that Harman and Ising were hiring people and suggested that I look them up about a job.

Fortunately, there were few traffic jams on Hollywood Boulevard in 1930. I was in a fever to follow this lead and piloted that Ford Coupe down the open road as fast as common sense and fellow vehicles allowed. Harman-Ising Studio turned out to be located on the second floor of a white stucco building on Hollywood Boulevard. A thriving little enterprise called Singer's Dress Shop occupied the first floor of the premises and a drugstore stood on the corner.

There was little protocol involved in this business of seeking a job. I simply entered the studio and asked the first person I met for work. I was taken to a man named Ray Katz who was apparently a kind of personnel director, and he introduced me to Hugh Harman and Rudolph Ising. A few moments later I had accepted a job offer from them working as a janitor for the studio at eighteen dollars a week.

The next day I went back to the Muller Brothers and told them about the job and apologized for leaving them after they had been good enough to give me work when I so desperately needed it. Sam looked at me and smiled. "Never mind, Bill. We just wanted to give you a leg up. Maybe you can get ahead working at a place like that." He jerked a thumb back to a couple of dusty automobiles waiting to be washed. "You're never going to get anywhere by working here and washing cars."

I looked at him gratefully and nodded. The Muller Brothers had given me a job when my prospects had been zero. But in the midst of this bleak Depression, an opportunity beckoned. Sam was right. His faith in me revived my spirits and I began to realize the challenge of living that awaited me was not merely survival of the fittest, but success for the fittest. Despite relentless national poverty, growing bread lines, and the heartbreaking uncertainty of the times, the practical confidence these plainspoken businessmen apparently had in me to get on with my life was like a hand laid on my shoulder. There still *were* places in life to go.

I shook hands with both my former benefactors and climbed back into my Ford Coupe and headed back to the Harman-Ising Studio. As I drove down Santa Monica Boulevard, I kept repeating to myself the names of my new employers: Harman-Ising. The combined sound of their two surnames appealed to my musical ear. "Harmonizing." I took it for a sign. You know the Irish are great believers in omens. Hopefully this one augured good fortune and an interesting future.

Chapter Two

East Meets West

H arman and Ising proved to be as amiable as their combined names suggested. They were both young men, still in their twenties, informally dressed in shirt-sleeves, and obviously enthusiastic about the business of making cartoons. Their little studio with its hallway of compact offices was a far cry from the high-tech complexes that produce animation cartoons today. It was modestly equipped with a camera, a movieola, and several intriguing-looking devices called lightboards. The latter were slanted drawing boards equipped with light bulbs which illuminated frosted glass panels, and were used by the animators for drawing cartoon illustrations depicting various stages of motion. In addition, there were some desks made of pine and fiberboard, one swivel chair, and not much else.

It was all pretty inexpensive equipment—it didn't cost a lot to equip an animation studio in those days. For a twenty-year-old kid fresh from the car wash, however, the set-up looked state of the art. Long paper panels depicting pencil sketches of backgrounds and drawings of cute animal characters were fastened with pushpins onto four-by-eight-foot panels of fiberboard attached to the walls.

Twenty years had passed since Winsor McCay first outlined similar drawings for his cartoon short *Little Nemo*. During those two decades the concept of animation had grown from such embryonic endeavors into an exciting fledgling industry. By the time I joined the

Harman-Ising Studio in 1930, the Walt Disney Studio had become the dominant force in American cartoonmaking.

Two years earlier, in 1928, Disney had featured a personable mouse named Mickey in a revolutionary cartoon called *Steamboat Willie* that proved the undeniable commercial appeal of cartoons made with sound. Both Hugh Harman and Rudolph Ising had worked as animators on Disney's original staff, but in 1929 ambitiously decided to create their own studio and forge careers as freelance producers of animated cartoons.

Such a display of entrepreneurial self-confidence in the teeth of a national depression by two men not much older than myself was both astonishing and inspiring to me. I soon became close friends with both Hugh and Rudy, and I think that their good-humored, optimistic belief in a bright future in animation production filled their entire little staff of about thirty animators and artists with the same hopeful expectations.

My first duties at Harman-Ising involved basic custodial tasks and running for coffee. I'd get to the studio around eight o'clock in the morning and by nine o'clock I'd have all the floors swept and the wastebaskets emptied. Shortly after joining the studio I was given a job washing the ink and paint off the acetate sheets used in cartoon production. This chore was generally done in a large sink. The sheets could then be re-used. A few weeks later, I was moved into the inking and painting department and soon assigned to run that unit. This primarily involved supervising a team of about seven girls who worked industriously at their tables detailing the color artwork on clear acetate film from nine o'clock in the morning to six o'clock in the evening with an hour off for lunch.

While I was running this small inking and painting department, I had a chance to observe firsthand everything that was involved in this seemingly complicated process of taking an idea in an artist's mind and seeing it take visual form on the screen as a humorous seven-minute animated cartoon.

The whole process generally began with a rough story idea worked up by either Hugh or Rudy. These ideas were often discussed between the two partners and story lines were developed. As the story evolved, one of the artists created a storyboard depicting each scene of the proposed cartoon. A storyboard is a kind of animation blueprint that consists of little three-by-four-inch sketches, numbering as many as seventy-five to a hundred drawings, that graphically tell the cartoon story from beginning to end and is used by almost everyone who is involved with the finished picture.

Generally the first people to refer to the storyboards in production were those in the model department. There, each character was designed and drawn in illustrations called model sheets. When the model sheets were approved by the director, they were then given to each animator involved in the production. When color was introduced in cartoons in the mid-1930s, it became necessary to formulate methods of insuring the quality of tone values as well as contrast. To achieve this, color models were painted to serve as guides indicating what colors were to be used on each character in the film. These character models were referred to by the animator and his assistant in order to maintain consistency of each character's appearance throughout the cartoon.

The finished drawings—about six thousand per seven-minute cartoon—were then checked to insure that they were properly drawn. They were then sent to the inking department, where the drawings were traced in black India ink on clear sheets of acetate film popularly referred to now as "cels."

From there, the cels were sent to the painting department, where color models were prepared of each character. There were about fifteen people at Harman-Ising painting the characters on the cels following the color markings indicated on the models.

The colored cels were then sent to the camera department where, with painted backgrounds, scenes were matched with the appropriate cels. The cameraman then photographed each cel according to the sequence of action to be depicted in the cartoon.

For each frame of film, a separate series of cels were placed over the same background and photographed in proper sequence. When all of the scenes were photographed, the film was processed and a print of the cartoon was viewed by the director to insure the consistency of quality of the film.

All in all, it was a very active and sociable environment. Everyone seemed to enjoy their work and each other and the family-like atmosphere at Harman-Ising set a personal precedent for me early on of discovering my closest friendships with the people with whom I worked. As partners, Hugh and Rudy were a study in contrasts. Hugh was the artist of the two, a very good animator with an outgoing personality. Rudy was a very quiet and private man who preferred to come into the studio in the afternoon and work late into the evening alone developing the story material for the cartoons.

Two of the characters featured in many of the early Looney Tunes and Merrie Melodies productions were Bosko and Honey, a little black boy and girl. These two characters at the time were competing with Walt Disney's Mickey Mouse for popularity with theatre audiences.

I was first introduced to the animated antics of Bosko and Honey shortly after joining the studio. I was able to view in the movieola (a small projector for dailies or short lengths of footage) the recently completed 35-mm print of one of their earliest cartoons for Warner Bros. called *Sinkin' in the Bathtub*. The engaging little slapstick gags coordinated with short, bright musical numbers appealed to me instantly. Rudy Ising's keen ability to conceive many ingenious little bits of comic business made his characters endearing and hilarious.

Rudy's work intrigued me, and I began to extend my work hours into the evenings to spend time with him. After putting in my day working with the inking and painting department, I would have my dinner and then come back to the studio and work with Rudy until about midnight developing material. At his encouragement, I began offering suggestions for possible gags or comic situations in the cartoons; whenever he thought any of these ideas might work, he used them. A lot of these things just came to me while I was working away painting a cel or maybe chewing on a ham sandwich at noon. They were generally zany little stunts typical of animated cartoons at that time and most often involved a prime Harman-Ising cartoon character like Bosko.

An example of the kind of gag I might have pitched to Hugh and Rudy in those days could have Bosko bouncing along on the back of his horse with only the reins in his hands. All of a sudden, the horse stops and little Bosko would fly over the horse, probably head over end, and *poosh*, land in a wooden tub head first in the water with a big splash. They were things like that: simple, slapstick action gags that would create a laugh. The work was fun and absorbing and I enjoyed the easy rapport that developed between Rudy and Hugh and myself as we brainstormed ideas for these Looney Tunes and Merrie Melodies pictures in a spirit of constant hilarity.

I also began writing little songs that Harman and Ising began to incorporate into the early Looney Tunes and Merrie Melodies cartoons. These lyrics were actually progressions of the whimsical little verses I had begun composing as a boy, never thinking at the time that they would ever lead to anything beyond maybe a family greeting card.

Combined with story development was the task of timing the action of the cartoon and synchronizing the animation with the music and sound effects. Having watched Hugh Harman direct the animation of many of their cartoons, I offered to assist him with the timing in some of these productions and he agreed to let me try. One of the key instruments that they employed in this process was a metronome. From my musical background, I knew how a metronome worked and I could figure out how many frames per beat were required for the precise coordination of action with sound. I also knew how to take these calculations and write them on music bar sheets which could be referred to in the direction of the cartoon. These bar sheets were similar to conventional sheet music, but were printed on a heavy grade of paper twelve inches high by twenty inches in width, and were used by the musicians to synchronize the cartoon's action with the music according to timing notations made by the director.

Timing a cartoon is a partly mathematical and partly intuitive process. In studying the markings indicated on the metronome, I was able to determine that when the metronome clicked at a rate of 144 beats per minute, every beat represented ten frames of film. Using the index of twenty-four frames a second in animation movement, I figured that a twelve beat was half of that, so every time it clicked it would be twelve frames. Using that multiple I marked on my metronome for a ten beat, twelve beat, fourteen beat, sixteen beat, and so on to setting the tempo of, for example, a character's walk by coordinating the action in frames to the beat of the metronome.

Such an axiom was fine for some things. In others, such as timing the facial reaction of a character, a double take, or some other comedic or dramatic bit of action, you just had to rely on your intuitive sense of timing and know how long you wanted to hold that look on their face, or other bit of business the action calls for. Then it becomes something that is *felt* more than precisely measured. You see it, you feel it, and somehow you just know if it is right or wrong.

The earliest sound cartoons employed a method of recording dialogue to the cartoon's animation. But this method had severe drawbacks. It often proved extremely restrictive to recording artists who provided the voices for the characters. In attempting to conform the reading of their lines to the specific movements of the animation, the actors often felt inhibited in their performance, and their vocal renditions often emerged stilted and awkward.

Fortunately, the flaws of this method were recognized early on. By the end of the 1930s the process was actually reversed, allowing the actors to record their lines first in as free and spontaneous a manner as they wished. The animation was then done to synchronize precisely with the vocals, resulting in a much more natural and livelier cartoon performance.

Hugh and Rudy were both extremely generous, giving me opportunities to gain a growing hands-on knowledge of animation production. I learned a lot from both men regarding the mechanics of making cartoons as well as an increased appreciation of the many subtle artistic and humorous nuances involved in creating appealing characters for personality animation. In return, I'd like to believe that my knowledge of music and rhythm applied to synchronizing animation scenes provided Hugh and Rudy a wider latitude of creative timing in their productions.

In many ways, the little staff at Harman-Ising functioned very much like the crew of a ship. During my apprenticeship at Harman-Ising, I had developed into a kind of pivot man who functioned in whatever aspect of production the two partners might require to get out the product. For the most part it had proved to be a remarkably congenial professional association, and I can recall only one instance of contention during my entire tenure at Harman-Ising.

Sometime during my third year running the inking and painting department, Rudy decided to hire his girlfriend, Irene Hamilton, to work in my unit as an inker. This was fine with me until I learned that she had been given a starting salary of sixty dollars a week! This was at a time when I was drawing a weekly paycheck of thirty-seven fifty. The blatant injustice of this arrangement raised my blood to the boiling point. After all, I reasoned, I had remained as the head of that department loyally committed to Hugh and Rudy for a long time and had worked my way up to a level where I felt I was performing many valuable production tasks.

Sheer necessity and my own self-respect demanded that I resolve this issue of just dues. Early one morning I drove over to the Disney Studio in Burbank and applied for a job as the head of their inking and painting department. That was my first introduction to Walt Disney. He listened gravely and without comment as I explained my dilemma at Harman-Ising.

When I had finished, Disney sat in silent deliberation for a few moments. "Well, I'll tell you, Bill," he said at last. "We already have a girl in our inking and painting department who's doing a hell of a good job. I suggest that you go back and tell Rudy about your problem and I'll bet you that you get your money."

It was well-intended advice and I decided to take it. I thanked

Disney for his time and headed back to Hollywood. I've always believed that Disney must have picked up the telephone and called Rudolph Ising after I left his office because when I returned to the studio, Rudy walked in to see me and said, "Bill, you're going to get your raise. From now on you'll be drawing sixty dollars a week."

During these early bachelor days, I roomed with one of the Harman-Ising artists, James Hezell. Jim was an Englishman who spoke with a very thick accent I enjoyed listening to, and in many ways he was a "right and proper" gent. He was an amiable enough guy and we got along all right, although he impressed me as having some distinct eccentricities. As long as I lived with him, I never knew Hezell to go out on a date or socialize with anyone. I did notice, however, that whenever he had a few extra dollars he was fond of going down to a Florsheim Shoe outlet located on Hollywood Boulevard and buying a new pair of shoes. He must have had at least seven or eight brand new pairs of shoes in his closet.

Hezell was a man definitely proud of his footgear. He may not have exactly fit the "all dressed up with no place to go" adage, but he certainly had the oxfords for the occasion. On Friday nights after work, Jim would open up the closet, take out all his shoes and lovingly apply another coat of polish to them. I watched this ritual silently a number of times until finally my curiosity got the better of me.

"Jim," I asked one evening, "what the hell gives with all these shoes? Every Friday night you take them out of the closet and spend all this time polishing them up!"

Hezell looked at me with ruffled indignation for a moment and then returned to his brushing and buffing. "Well," he replied. "A fellow's got to have some recreation in his life, doesn't he?"

Recreation, I imagine, is primarily a subjective idea, as individual as people themselves. I can remember my early internship years in animation production being a time of sheer and absolute recreation. I had fun doing what I was doing and the excitement of the work generally energized rather than fatigued me. The conventional nine-to-five or other eight-hour-shift employment arrangements were alien concepts to me. Very often, my evening sessions with Rudy concluded workdays which ran as long as fourteen or fifteen hours.

This was all, of course, elective on my part. I continued to visit my parents and sisters frequently at home on weekends, and on occasion I took a girlfriend out on a date. My recent raise in pay enabled me to supplement my parents' income and to also move into a larger apartment that I occupied alone. I also had a little more money that enabled me to occasionally enjoy the nightlife by taking a girl out to dinner and later maybe to the movies (complete with animated cartoons), or maybe to one of the local Hollywood nightclubs to listen to such popular musical artists of the time as Fats Waller and his orchestra.

I had found my life's calling at last. Every aspect of animation production enthralled me and seemed to provide me with a satisfying channel for creative expression. Just barely twenty-one years old, I decided that I would be blissfully happy if I could make cartoons for the rest of my life. In the midst of this serene revelation, however, a shadow fell on our little studio that soberly reminded us of the uncertain fortunes that plague any industry, including that of making cartoons.

Sometime in the middle of 1933, Leon Schlesinger decided to terminate his business relationship with Harman-Ising and independently produce his own cartoons directly for Warner Brothers. In this severance, Schlesinger took most of the Harman-Ising employees with him. By this time, I had developed a deep friendship for both Hugh and Rudy and elected to remain with them in the hope and belief that they would obtain new contracts for producing animation and we could carry on together.

While Harman-Ising negotiated with other production houses for work, a small core of Hugh and Rudy's staff along with myself, who were now virtually unemployed, struggled to make ends meet. For several weeks we tightened our belts and free-lanced for whatever meager work that was available. Occasionally we would be able to get little jobs animating commercials for advertising agencies. It wasn't much but we were able to survive. We were sustained in great part during this period by the generosity of the owner of Peters' Drugstore, which stood close by our studio.

Knowing the tight spot we were all in at that time, Mr. Peters magnanimously ran a tab for our little crew that allowed us to eat at the drugstore for very little money. For about fifteen cents we would be able to get a breakfast of a bowl of cereal, and for about thirty-five cents you could get an adequate supper of a plate of spaghetti or maybe a serving of liver and onions.

Fortunately, our summer of discontent ended after about three months when Harman and Ising signed a contract producing cartoons directly for Metro-Goldwyn-Mayer Studio. We were rolling again. Hugh and Rudy were back at the helm, and both men were providing me with ample opportunities to begin piloting my own course. I was about twenty-three years old and my enthusiasm was running high. My professional initiation into animation production had come by degrees, but it had also rapidly advanced in a relatively short time.

Hugh and Rudy were both deeply appreciative of the loyalty shown by the handful of artists and animators who had elected to remain with them during that uncertain period. Once they had gotten their new contract I was placed in the story department and given an opportunity to work with Hugh in developing material for new cartoons. Eventually, Harman and Ising extended my creative boundaries even further by providing me with opportunities to make some cartoons on my own. I was then able to utilize all the acquired skills of writing, animating, and timing to direct my own projects.

One of my first endeavors in cartoon production was an effort called *To Spring*, which I did in association with a wonderfully gifted artist named Paul Fennell. Unlike many of the comic cartoons being produced at the time, *To Spring* was what one might call a straight piece intended to provide for viewers what is often referred to today as a "visual feast for the eyes." Since I prided myself as having a green thumb in gardening, I decided to apply my animation skills toward making flowers blossom in a seven-minute cartoon celebrating spring. The artwork in this picture was stunning and featured a colorful sequence of images of blooming roses, lilies, tulips, and other assorted flora.

The teamwork involved in this production under my supervision was extremely gratifying and somewhat awesome to me. After all, here I was, this young kid who had been lucky enough to find a job he thoroughly enjoyed doing and getting paid for it, finding himself now working with a studio full of veteran talents earnestly applying their skills to the development of his own project. Hugh and Rudy had been excellent tutors. Production went smoothly with each aspect of development leading my little premier cartoon closer to its full evolution as a completed product for release to a genuine audience.

And then one afternoon, it was done. There it was in my hands, a tightly wound reel of flammable nitrate stock ready for viewing on our movieola. The staff was already industriously absorbed in another production. I ran the film on our projector and it began to spin off the series of images which we had all frame by frame carefully timed and crafted for weeks. The title appeared, and there in the flickering small screen of our movieola a moment later, the credits including an astonishing phrase: "Directed by William Hanna."

I was a happy man. These, as they say, "were the salad days of my youth," and I was as green as springtime. I had two mentors who were providing me with the opportunities to learn my craft, hone my creative skills, and master them, if I was capable, while assisting Hugh and Rudy to answer the rigorous production demands of their hard-won contract with MGM Studio. Despite earnest efforts, Harman and Ising had gained a reputation of being notoriously slow in delivering the required quota of cartoons to MGM, and Hugh and Rudy hoped that my directorial projects, along with their own projects, could effectively increase their volume of production.

All in all, it was a very good time for me to be alive. The Depression, of course, always loomed as an ominous but somewhat vague threat, for although my family and I were always careful and conservative with our money, we never suffered the grinding poverty that devastated so many other Americans during those years. This was a blessing, however, that none of us ever took for granted. The crisis demanded that I constantly seek new windows of opportunity to better the welfare of the family.

A few years after joining Harman-Ising, I was able to secure jobs for two of my sisters, Evelyn and Jessilee, painting cels at our studio. In a recent conversation with my sisters, Evelyn remembered me bringing home celluloid sheets, paint brushes, and paints and earnestly informing them that I was going to teach them an important job skill in the animation business. Happily, they both proved to be adept students as well as fine artists who went on to enjoy good careers as artists at both Warner Bros. and Walt Disney studios.

God Almighty and the cartoon industry had been good to us. We ate well and slept warmly and, what's more, beyond the protective insulation of family love and parental approval, I had what discerning elders of the day called "prospects." I had hitched my wagon to a rising star called the cartoon business with a fervent faith that that star would not prove to be a bright but short-lived meteorite blazing into obscurity.

One of my pals at Harman-Ising at that time was a writer by the name of Mo Caldwell. Mo was going with a girl by the name of Vera Wogatzke and seemed to be getting along with her pretty well. One evening, Mo mentioned that Vera had a twin sister by the name of Violet and suggested that we all go out on a double date. I agreed and a few nights later was introduced to a petite, brown-haired girl who would shortly afterward become the wife to whom I have been happily married for the past fifty-nine years.

This realization did not consciously dawn upon me at our first meeting. At least, I don't think it did. I was a pretty relaxed bachelor and not particularly shy. Dating to me then was primarily a decorous, although enjoyable, social ritual that I still regarded as a casual recess from the real serious business of life, which was making cartoons. It did not take long to realize, however, that although Violet Wogatzke was one of two very attractive twin sisters, she was also quite impressively a distinct and unique individual in her own right.

Despite the fact that she was three years younger than me, I found Violet to be an exceptionally bright, self-assured, and independent young woman. She had been living on her own for some time when we met, and worked as a secretary for a Los Angeles insurance company. Like myself, she came from a large and close-knit family, and I was impressed by the fact that she diligently reserved a part of her paycheck so that she could send money home every week to her parents at their ranch in Imperial Valley, California.

Vi soon became an invaluable creative consultant regarding my work. She took an immediate and intense interest in my career in animation and often critiqued my work as I continued to develop story material and gags for new cartoons. As a sounding board, she proved to be both perceptive and candid in her opinions, and she would both praise and criticize my professional efforts with a kind but clear eye.

Although I had grown up amidst an abundance of females in my family and dated numerous young women, I had never met a girl quite like Violet. She neither resembled my mother nor any of my sisters in personality or appearance, although she shared many of their family values. My relationship with Violet, however, brought another dimension of realization to me regarding women, and that was a growing awareness of what I've sometimes heard people refer to as "feminine mystique."

This is a very elusive thing, and very difficult if not impossible (at least for men) to describe, but I would imagine that it is one of the major energy sources that has kept the world turning for a very long time. Our courtship lasted for about a year. On August 7, 1936, we were married in a simple ceremony at Immaculate Conception Church with a restaurant reception on Hollywood Boulevard. Shortly after the wedding, we drove to San Pedro and, taking the car with us, sailed up to San Francisco, where we disembarked and drove north to the Sierra Nevada for a two-week honeymoon at Lake Tahoe.

When I returned to work I continued to pursue opportunities to direct my own cartoons. I had a wife now with whom I shared exciting plans to eventually buy and build our own home. Hugh and Rudy were more than willing to provide me with opportunities to direct and even produce my own cartoons in order to help meet the production demands stipulated in their contract with MGM.

Whenever I study one of the photographs taken of our staff at Harman-Ising so many years ago, I continue to be amazed at the amount of exceptionally talented people we had assembled in that little group. We were a good professional unit and extremely fond of each other. I would have been happy to spend the rest of my life producing cartoons with Harman-Ising Studio, but as it turned out, that halcyon period was rapidly drawing to a close.

Despite our combined production activities, Harman and Ising were unable to maintain an adequate supply of cartoons to meet MGM's contractual demands. Unhappy over the cost overruns on Harman-Ising cartoons, MGM decided in 1937 to cancel their contract with Hugh and Rudy and to form its own cartoon studio. Admittedly, Harman-Ising found themselves in a situation where they had over-committed themselves in cartoon production to MGM, but from a larger perspective, such a development also indicated the dramatic growth of the entire animation industry.

The demand for quality animated cartoons had increased significantly in recent years and competition among such major studios as Disney, Warner Bros., Screen Gems, and MGM to capture large theatre-going audiences was spirited and intense. The days of subcontractors producing cartoons for large studios was on the wane, and many of the larger film companies were striving to emulate the Disney Studio's production volume of popular animation properties.

The termination of Harman-Ising's contractual relationship with MGM signaled another possible disruption in all of our professional lives. I had worked with Hugh and Rudy during the formative professional years of my youth and we had remained good friends. But an era had ended and a new one beckoned.

The news of MGM's termination with Harman and Ising fell like a thunderbolt on our studio. This was the second time in my seven-year association with Hugh and Rudy that we had had the rug pulled out from under us. It was an unhappy reversal of fortune.

Once again a major lay-off loomed threateningly; somewhat stunned, we all could not help but wonder if our impending unemployment might turn into an indefinite struggle for survival.

In the midst of this grim speculation, I received a telephone call from the head of MGM's cartoon department, Fred Quimby, which set my heart racing. Quimby had evidently been impressed by the recently run *To Spring,* and had noticed my directorial credit. MGM had given Quimby the job of running their new cartoon unit and he was now in the midst of recruiting an in-house animation production staff. As part of his effort to accomplish this he invited me and several other Harman-Ising employees to a dinner one evening and proposed that we join MGM and assist in the formation of its cartoon studio.

As I recall, we were all unanimous in our acceptance of Quimby's offer. Bob Allen and myself were hired as directors of animation. Max Maxwell was made production manager. I felt that this change was not only critical to my career in animation, but the possible threshold to dramatic personal creative growth as well. Fred Quimby and MGM had invited us to help build something new and ambitious in the cartoon business. We were challenged to be more than artists and animators working at our drawing boards. If we did our jobs right, we would be creating the architecture of a young studio that could become a major contender in commercial animation.

I excitedly discussed the prospects with my wife, Vi, who staunchly upheld my decision to join MGM. We rented a small apartment on Olympic Boulevard in Los Angeles in order to be closer to the studio and shortly afterward, I made my first drive to work at a studio where I was to spend the next twenty years. MGM had staked its claim on a lot of real estate in Culver City and by 1937 showed ample evidence of growing into the sprawling production complex it eventually became.

Our embryonic cartoon studio, however, was at first a modest little building set on MGM's Lot 2, adjacent to the regular motion picture studio. Our first day there was somewhat like a high school reunion, for many of the Harman-Ising alumni had been hired by Quimby as part of the core unit. On the following day, a second contingent of storymen and animators arrived at MGM from New York. It was an interesting day for all of us. Californians met New Yorkers as we were introduced to the East coast people Quimby had recruited including Dan and George Gordon, Ray Kelly, Paul Sommer, and Joe Barbera. Fred Quimby now had his cartoon studio complete, with a talented assembly of animators, artists, and writers who all seemed to have that hungry, eager look of young Turks in a new arena.

I believe it was Rudyard Kipling who once said, "East is East and West is West, and never the twain shall meet." With all due respect to literary maxims, however, I have through time and experience come to rely upon a personal aphorism which I've often applied at many of life's thresholds: You can often, when the occasion merits, create an exception to the rule.

Chapter Three

The Great Chase

Fred Quimby had done a good job in assembling a promising corps of animation talent for MGM. Right from the outset, however, it became apparent to most of us that, although Quimby had laid the foundation for this infant studio, he expected his new recruits to provide the creative mortar for its construction. Unlike Harman and Ising, Quimby was never what you would call a hands-on producer of animation.

Fred had acquired a fine and long service record with MGM as a loyal executive and extremely competent film distributor for the company in New York. As a reward for his many years of service, he was given the job of running our cartoon studio and brought out to the West Coast. Fred was in his early fifties when I first met him, although he looked many years older. He was always immaculately attired in expensively tailored suits that seemed to impart more dignity than dash to his appearance, presenting the image of a solid and benevolent elder businessman. It was an image entirely appropriate to Fred's character.

Most of us in the department were still in our twenties and many years younger than Quimby. Characteristic of both our youth and our profession, we were in general an informal group of kids dressed in slacks and shirt-sleeves that did not always escape the India ink, graphite, or paint stains that are the inevitable marks of animators and artists thoroughly engrossed in their work.

Although Quimby respected this creative intimacy, he did not share it. Fred was the executive. It was our job to turn out the product, and it was Quimby's job to make sure that we got it done. How we did it was a creative concern that he pretty much left us to work out on our own. This did not by any means imply indifference to our efforts on Quimby's part, for he was very proud of and entirely committed to the business success of our newly inaugurated animation studio. But Fred's forte was distributing the product. He simply did not understand anything about animation production and was unable to comprehend either the abstract or the technical challenges involved in the process of creating cartoons.

In order to insure production efficiency, Quimby had hired a veteran Disney artist named Max Maxwell as his production manager. Maxwell had gone on from Disney's to work as a production manager at Harman-Ising and was an extremely capable supervisor with a confident and clear grasp of every aspect of animation production. What's more, Max also understood the creative temperament of the people involved in cartoonmaking and acted as an effective communication liaison between ourselves and Fred Quimby.

The MGM cartoon studio in those earliest days was in many ways a microcosm of the democratic concept of our own national free enterprise system. The artistic staff assembled there formed a virtual melting pot of creative personalities. Included on Quimby's roster of talents were such gifted people as Friz Freleng, Tex Avery, and Irven Spence. All of them brought to a single studio their own distinct and varied *modus operandi* of cartoon production.

I personally grew to develop a great affection for Fred Quimby. I respected him for his integrity and administrative poise and wanted to validate his confidence in our production potential. My first directorial assignment from the MGM brass, however, did not provide an auspicious beginning toward that end. Metro-Goldwyn-Mayer had purchased the rights to a comic strip called "The Katzenjammer Kids" and decided to turn the property into a series of animated pictures which they retitled "The Captain and the Kids." Now, "The Katzenjammer Kids" was a popular comic strip, but I had immediate grave misgivings about whether we could successfully convert these somewhat ponderously drawn human characters along with their German accents into a successful cartoon.

It had been a poor selection for animation development, and those of us involved with the task of putting it on the screen knew it. That was the job we had been given, however, and we earnestly set out to do the best we could in producing an appealing film. The results were a dismal disappointment. Despite being beautifully animated, The Captain and the Kids series failed to endear themselves to a theatre audience. The artwork, although faithfully reproduced from parent drawings, did not translate well onto film, and the characters somehow lacked the warmth and lovable quality so necessary for popular cartoon personalities.

Despite my frustration with this endeavor, however, working on The Captain and the Kids reinforced and sharpened my personal concept of what I intuitively felt was the winning combination of elements essential to the creation of an enduring and endearing animation product. To begin with, you needed appealing characters who possessed a kind of visual cartoon charisma. Cuteness was often a part of this charisma, as I had learned from my years with Hugh and Rudy. In addition to their visual appeal, however, it was necessary to provide storylines that would virtually rock with hilarity and were enhanced with maybe just a touch of cunning and subtle irony tossed in for creative intrigue. In order for these elements to come across, it was necessary to virtually orchestrate the action sequences as well as the music and other sound elements in an animated coordination requiring precise timing.

I had developed a feel for all these production factors during my internship years with Harman-Ising, but here at MGM the heat of competition from rival studios producing animation compelled a lot of us to try and put a high gloss on this process and work something up that would be new, original, and a real contender for supreme cartoon stardom.

In the meantime, MGM executives continued to promote The Captain and the Kids in an obstinate bid for audience acceptance. Bob Allen, Friz Freleng, and I were all assigned to direct individual cartoons for the series and we were all bombing in our efforts. For six months we worked an average of fifty hours a week in a heated endeavor to direct this uncongenial property into a hit series. It was no go. We were chopping, but no chips were flying. According to the reports of theatre owners relayed to Fred Quimby, the series was simply not getting the laughs from the audience. The Captain and the Kids became to all of us a kind of production albatross and

I soon became convinced that it never would fly as a successful animation endeavor.

I've heard it said that in every adversity is the seed of a greater advantage. As I pecked away for such a hopeful kernel, the toil involved in my work at this time forced me to admit that a great part of my personal frustration during those months stemmed from a growing awareness of some of my own professional limitations. Eight years of striving to meet all of the creative demands of efficient animation production had, with the refinement of many skills, also rewarded me with the realization that I was a lousy artist.

During the earliest years of my career, I had consoled my personal disappointment over these drafting failures with a growing confidence in the creative talents I knew I had in composing music and lyrics and in animation timing and direction. While still working at Harman-Ising I had often been fortunate at being able to enlist talented artists such as Paul Fennell, with whom I worked to turn out cartoons for Hugh and Rudy. But that was at a time when I was still primarily a hired hand with growing aspirations.

It was a different ballgame at MGM. I was employed as a director now and allied with a platoon of some of the most prominent and established cartoon producers in the industry. Individually, we were all confronted with the same challenge of developing a seamless production unit that could produce winning cartoon products with consistent efficiency. That was the deal that brought us all to MGM and I knew that if I wanted to keep working, I would have to deliver the goods, *and soon.*

By the time I'd completed my third or fourth feature for the floundering Captain series, I knew that I had reached a juncture in my career. I came to the realization that at the age of twenty-eight I would have to obtain two things that were critically essential to my professional fulfillment. The first was a decent cartoon property that I could really get my teeth into. If such a concept could not be acquired, well, then Mother Necessity would have to invent one. The other conclusion I drew was that I would have to find a creatively inspired partner who was also a distinctly talented artist.

One might believe that a young animation studio filled with ambitious comers would have provided an ample roster of candidates. In all truthfulness, I never considered anyone except the man with whom I would eventually work for over five eventful decades. Among the artists who had arrived at MGM from New York during our first week at the studio was a dark-haired youth with a voluble personality named Joe Barbera.

Joe had grown up in the Flatbush section of New York and as a boy had developed an early passion for the theatre and acting. He also discovered that he had a remarkable flair for writing and drawing, which he actively pursued as a student at Erasmus High School in Brooklyn.

Joe had felt the staggering impact of the Depression in the East as much as I had in the West, and upon graduating from high school had found himself on the streets without a job. With pluck and persistence, he was finally able to find work in a bank filing income tax returns for the Irving Trust Company on Wall Street.

His real dream, however, was to become a commercial artist. During his lunch hours, he would make the rounds at the editorial offices of such major uptown publications as *The New Yorker* and *Redbook*, depositing cartoons he had drawn and hoped to sell, only to have to retrieve the rejected work the following week. Joe was eventually able to sell some of his drawings to *Collier's* magazine and doggedly pursued his quest of becoming a professional artist by taking courses at the Pratt Institute.

Shortly afterward, Joe landed a job painting and inking cels for the Fleischer Studios, which had originated the animation characters Betty Boop and Popeye the Sailor. Ambitious as well as talented, it took Joe less than a week working at the Fleischer Studios to realize that the chances for professional advancement there were about as scarce as orchids in a cornfield. When he learned that a man in his thirties had been working at the same job inking cels for three years at a wage of thirty-five dollars a week, the nineteen year old aspiring artist decided to quit his job and seek his prospects elsewhere.

Following a tip from a former fraternity friend from Erasmus, Joe applied for and got a job as an animator at the Van Beuren Studio in Manhattan, but his apparent talents as a writer soon led him to the story department. During those early days, there wasn't a hell of a lot of job security involved in animation production. My own experiences with layoffs at Harman-Ising and the eventual closing of their studio had taught me that. Joe endured many of the same vicissitudes at the beginning of his own career on the opposite end of the country. In 1936, the Van Beuren Studio lost its distributor, RKO Pictures, when the latter signed a contract to make cartoons for the Walt Disney Studio. Van Beuren was forced to close its studio and go out of business and once again, Joe found himself unemployed.

One afternoon while visiting a friend at Paul Terry's Studio in New Rochelle, Joe met Paul Terry, an independent producer who was producing theatrical cartoons, and accepted a job working on his Terrytoons. Terry would in later years give audiences such popular characters as Mighty Mouse, Heckle and Jeckle and Deputy Dawg. While working at the Terry Studio, Joe became close friends with another animator named Jack Zander. In mid-1937, Zander received a phone call from Max Maxwell inviting him and his fellow artists to join the newly formed staff of the MGM cartoon studio. Zander passed the news on to Joe and, joined by several other colleagues, they promptly made the eager migration to California.

Joe's remarkable artistic talents were apparent to me from virtually our first introduction. I could see that he possessed the ability to capture mood and expression in a quick sketch better than anyone else I knew. He was also brimming with ideas for working up clever cartoon gags which appealed to my own sense of humor. Joe originally joined MGM with the option of becoming either a writer or an animator. His creative writing talents were soon recognized by Friz Freleng, who hired him to work in his production unit as a story man.

Friz Freleng was a veteran director who had worked as an animator with Walt Disney and gone on to gain great prominence for his directorial achievements at Warner Bros., where his production of lively "musical show business" cartoons became one of his distinct creative trademarks. Freleng had recently accepted an offer by Quimby to leave Warner Bros. and join MGM with the hope of being given the opportunity to create some new cartoon concepts of his own. As it turned out, Freleng was assigned the task of producing The Captain and the Kids and Joe found himself involved with Friz, myself and a number of other guys who were working on what he called an "animated turkey."

Freleng became so disenchanted with this series that he shortly afterward left MGM and rejoined Warner Bros. Quimby, acknowledging at last the failure of The Captain and the Kids, decided to cancel the series. He conceded that we were free to try and develop new cartoon concepts on our own. The bright optimism of Quimby's executive staff regarding our studio's prospects for success began to dim, and consternation grew as the critical need of their company to deliver a fresh and original hit cartoon concept to distributors remained an appalling frustration. In a further attempt to remedy this dilemma, Quimby invited Hugh Harman and Rudy Ising to rejoin their colleagues at the studio in the hope that they would be able to provide the desperately needed hit.

Hugh and Rudy both accepted Quimby's offer, and upon their arrival at the studio promptly proceeded to establish independent production units of their own. For those of us still striving to hit our stride as able competitors of the old guards at Warners and Disney, these startling turnovers were becoming a professional game of musical chairs, and all for the sake of the ardent quest for the right cartoon.

Joe Barbera and I soon found ourselves sitting opposite each other in the story department, working with Rudy Ising. Rudy was developing an animation property in the form of a character called Barney Bear. There were a lot of chefs in the kitchen and each was working on his own brand of soup. Separate units evolved from individual and diverse production concepts. Tex Avery, one of Warner's most prolific directors, joined MGM at this time; like Harman and Ising, he proceeded to establish a self-contained production team that he ran with autonomous efficiency.

I was admiring and somewhat envious of these veterans. Guys like Friz, Tex, Hugh, and Rudy had already achieved artistic distinction for their animation production achievements, and their work bore the definite imprint of their own individual identities. They were not only colleagues but respectable role models as well.

Working with these guys produced a high-pressure creative environment which challenged me to somehow deliver a product that would carry its own distinctive hallmark. I had given myself a tall order, and to achieve it would require a team effort. Although I was not aware of it at the time, Joe Barbera was apparently nursing similar aspirations.

Working with Rudy Ising gave Joe and me ample opportunity to ponder how we might create original cartoon concepts of our own. The production pace Rudy had set for the development of his Barney Bear cartoons seemed almost leisurely to me. Joe and I more often than not were left alone in the same room to bounce ideas off each other in eager discussion. As I recall, we considered a lot of different combinations for a possible winning team of cartoon characters. One of the major elements guiding this selection was, of course, the nature of the relationship between the principles. We eventually agreed that the cartoon's action would be the liveliest and the most humorous if it was generally sparked by an ongoing conflict between the characters.

In order for this to work, the critters we picked would have to be natural adversaries like a dog and a cat, or a bird and a cat. We eventually settled on a cat and a mouse, and I've got to admit that this selection did not exactly produce an ovation for originality among any of our coworkers. Cat and mouse combinations were a staple in the cartoon business. Virtually every other cartoon studio had come up with their own version, including Disney, Terrytoons, and Walter Lantz Productions.

No one appeared to take our endeavor seriously at the time, but Joe and I were undismayed. Joe's initial sketches of our proposed characters were among the most appealing in animation that I had ever seen, and I believe that we were both convinced that we could come up with a clever set of cartoon personalities with a charisma all their own.

The cat, which we decided to call Jasper, was of course cast as the heavy, and he looked every bit the part in those first drawings. Joe had drawn Jasper in a way that gave the cat a mangy, villainous look that made him appear downright menacing. The mouse, in contrast, was a diminutive, wide-eyed victim we named Jinx. I could tell from Joe's first sketches that the variety of expressions and attitudes he was able to impart with his pencil to both characters promised something very special.

With the other units at the studio completely absorbed in developing their own respective properties, Joe and I were pretty much left alone to proceed on our project without interference. For two months the two of us sat at the same desk, facing each other, and excitedly discussed ideas for the development of the story material for Jinx and Jasper. There was no scriptwriting involved in these sessions. The gags and story action were simply worked out on storyboards after we had voiced our ideas regarding the cartoon's concept.

During these conversations, Joe would dexterously draw sketch after sketch of a whole series of humorous situations that virtually seemed to animate themselves in a sequence of ingenious pencil illustrations. Studying these panels as they emerged on paper, I think we both sensed that we were really onto something. The quest for what would hopefully be the introduction of new cartoon celebrities had led us to a traditional but hilarious, rambunctious, and suspenseful game of cat and mouse. The great chase was on.

This first creative collaboration between Joe Barbera and myself resulted in a seven-minute cartoon called *Puss Gets the Boot*. During the production of this film, Joe and I availed ourselves of the opportunity to experiment with a number of innovative animation techniques. One of these methods involved elaborating on a concept called a pose reel. The pose reel was a preliminary test film used during that period as a kind of blueprint for the finished cartoon. It was actually an abbreviated version of the cartoon and consisted primarily of selected storyboard sketches of key poses and extreme shots. These were photographed and set to a pre-recorded soundtrack and when viewed, would give the illusion of action in a limited form. Joe and I decided to elaborate on this pose reel concept; we expanded the test film to include more drawings to get a better feel for refining the finished product.

Unlike conventional pose reels, our test film contained initial drawings created by Joe that were very detailed illustrations and contained indications for various camera shots including notations for close-ups, long shots, and pans. This provided us with what amounted to a layout of the whole picture to be animated. In addition, we resorted to such improvisations as shaking the camera or using zoom shots to simulate the reel's animation to a more convincing degree. I then took those drawings and timed the picture to synchronize the images to the film's action. When we had done all of that, we sent the layout drawings to the camera department to be photographed. Then we prepared to preview our ambitious seven-minute prototype to the studio executives.

When Quimby and his staff entered the projection room, they looked more than a little dubious over whether this thing might go over. A few minutes later, however, the room was literally rocking with laughter as the clattering film in the movieola spun out a series of frantic chases and mischievous antics of two precocious characters that we hoped might prove to be a winning cartoon duo for MGM.

So far so good. Our test film had indicated the potential for a good cartoon. What the studio brass was really concerned with, however, was public reaction to the finished product. Jinx and Jasper still had to overcome the stigma of being typecast as conventional cat and mouse characters. They would have to sell themselves to our theatre audiences as original personalities in their own right. Could they do it? Could *we* do it?

Puss Gets the Boot was released to theatres in February of 1940. Since we were both still rookie directors among many veteran producers, neither one of us had as yet acquired much studio clout, and the production credit for *Puss Gets the Boot* went to our unit supervisor, Rudolph Ising. Joe and I took this philosophically and shrugged it off. What the hell else was there to do? Still, we both had high hopes for our product, and aspirations of developing the characters into contenders for their own series.

But Fred Quimby's skepticism over the premier picture's prospects overruled us, and we were directed to cease from working on any more cat and mouse films. This was a jarring blow to us, but Joe and I were both young and down to our fighting weight. By this time, we had both sensed that the creative symbiosis that sparked our production teamwork might prove to have some real staying power in our careers and we agreed to continue working together as partners. Reluctantly conceding to Quimby's veto, we swallowed our disappointment and went back to the drawing board still stubbornly resolved to come up with new candidates for hit cartoon characters.

Despite the apparently abundant gallery of popular animation personalities familiar to the public today, the creation of such enduring inkwell celebrities like Mickey Mouse or Daffy Duck is a rare phenomenon. For every Felix the Cat, Bugs Bunny, or Woody Woodpecker that has ascended into cartoon folklore there were virtually hundreds, even thousands, of artists' and writers' concepts of similar felines, rabbits, birds, and other species fated to failure and obscurity. Joe and I knew we were bucking the odds, but we were determined to beat them. What's more, the league of elite veterans at our studio had proven that it could be done.

Friz Freleng and Tex Avery had achieved this at Warner Bros. with the development of a hugely successful ensemble cast of characters including Bugs Bunny, Daffy Duck, and Porky Pig. Hugh Harman and Rudy Ising had pioneered early Merrie Melodies and Looney Tunes characters. Yes, it could be done, and in their own way all of these veterans had in some way done it. None of them, however, had yet achieved this at MGM.

Our next collaborative efforts were disappointments to both Joe and myself. We came up with two new offerings, a cartoon involving gossiping mares at a racetrack called *Gallopin' Gals*, and a second picture which featured a canine character named Officer Pooch. *Gallopin' Gals* and *Officer Pooch* provided their share of humorous gags and engaging artwork, but the characters lacked the chemistry, magic, and screen presence of our cat and mouse duo.

During this time, *Puss Gets the Boot* had been running in theatres and, as it was turning out, making quite a splash with audiences. Joe and I were still rooting for the team, and our loyalty to our first animated creation remained undiminished. I can remember often driving by a theatre on Wilshire Boulevard in Los Angeles where the cartoon ran for several weeks and breathing a silent benediction for our cartoon contenders as the audience bought their tickets for the show. "Knock 'em dead, fellas!" I would exhort. "Break a leg, make 'em roar, and above all, win their hearts!"

Do cartoon characters assume an intelligence of their own upon their birth on the screen? After all, they move, react, and assume distinct personalities. If they are good characters, they even go beyond that dimension to establish relationships with their human audiences. Perhaps there is a little Pinnochio in every true cartoon creation, where the character at some point emerges from illusion to assume a real-life personality of its own.

Yes, Virginia, there is a God in Heaven, and I believe that he likes cartoons. One afternoon Joe and I were asked to come to Fred Quimby's office. Apparently, MGM executives were impressed by the enthusiastic public response to *Puss Gets the Boot*. When they received a letter from a major theatre distributor inquiring when the studio was going to make more of "those delightful cat and mouse cartoons," the staff began to look at Jinx and Jasper with a new light of admiration in their eyes.

Suddenly, cat and mouse teams gained a new respectability. They were no longer a tired and stale format but "a tried and true concept given an original new treatment." Well, we could have told them that all along. As it turned out, Rudy Ising, who had been preoccupied with producing Barney Bear, had remained pretty detached from our activities during the time Joe and I had developed *Puss Gets the Boot*. Consequently, it was conceded that Joe and I were the creators of the characters of this film. To our elation, we were directed to continue on our own as a team to produce a new series featuring our original cat and mouse duo.

Aspiring inventors are often advised that if you build a new mousetrap, the world will beat a path to your door. In our situation, we were hoping for pretty much the opposite. Success for Joe and me meant that our little mouse would be running for a long time and that his escape was always assured. If things went well, the little bastard would never get caught. Well, not for very long, anyway.

Chapter Four

The Good New Days

Although MGM was a relative latecomer to introducing a commercially successful animation series to the market, it lost no time in gaining the respect of competitors for producing cartoon films of artistic distinction. In 1939, at the outbreak of World War II, our studio released at Christmas time a cartoon with a strong pacifist theme entitled *Peace On Earth*. Produced by Hugh Harman, the film was a beautifully crafted allegory of mankind's final destructive conflict with itself, and was nominated for an Academy Award. I was tremendously moved by the emotional impact of Hugh's production and, although I didn't realize it at the time, the film would many years later have a significant influence on both my and Joe Barbera's career.

To our amazement, *Puss Gets the Boot* was also nominated for an Academy Award in 1940. Somewhat incredulously, Joe and I thanked our lucky stars for this professional affirmation. We directed our gratitude not to heavenly bodies, but rather to the fortunate renderings of our feline and rodent personalities—who now seemed on the brink of becoming celebrities.

During some earnest discussion, Joe and I decided to refine the artwork of the characters in order to enhance their audience appeal. The villainy of the cat was softened by giving him a sleeker form and a less sinister expression. The mouse was also given a makeover and redrawn as a cuter, cuddlier, chubby-cheeked fellow, rather than the lean little fugitive who had appeared in our first film.

As we worked to spruce up these characters for their anticipated stardom, one thing continued to bother us. A winning team needed a winning name, and "Jasper and Jinx" just did not seem to fit the bill. We needed something that would sing in the tradition of such famous and phonetically pleasing name combinations as Lewis and Clark, or Gilbert and Sullivan, or, for that matter, Laurel and Hardy. At length, we came upon something that suited both of us. Tom and Jerry. I cannot honestly recall which one of us originally suggested the names, but I do remember that before we could toast the success of this new team, we had to secure legal consent for them to adopt their new identities from the famous drink (a rum and eggnog Christmas concoction).

At any rate, permission was granted, and our refurbished cat and mouse, neé Jasper and Jinx, were officially rechristened Tom and Jerry. Their first appearance under these names was in *The Midnight Snack*, produced in 1941. The film was basically a refinement of the original chase premise in *Puss Gets the Boot*, only employing better gag material. This was followed by *The Night Before Christmas*, which was released to theatres at the end of 1941.

I've always had a warm spot in my heart for this cartoon. The storyline added extra dimension to the relationship of our two characters by showing Tom, who is comfortably sheltered in a warm house, compassionately concerned for Jerry, who is outside freezing to death. The picture was a heartwarming little story filled with Yuletide spirit and astonished Joe and me by winning us our second Academy Award nomination.

One of the things that Joe and I agreed upon early on was that we would create our cat and mouse as mute personalities whose humorous appeal would be communicated through the eloquence of their physical movements rather than dialogue (although we planned to sometimes include dialogue from supporting characters to enhance the plot). In this way we parted company with the artistic methods employed by the guys at Warner Bros., for example. They relied primarily on the wisecrack and distinctive voice characterizations to provide characters such as Bugs Bunny or Daffy Duck their personal brands of wit and personality. Pantomime is a universal language of humor that loses nothing through translation. The zips, scrambles, chases, falls, fights, and frolics of Tom and Jerry could be laughed at and appreciated by anyone who could identify with human frailties, daily dilemmas, and the overall absurdities of life. Whatever verbal effects were employed were generally basic yowls, ouches, screams, roars, or sobs that we thought were just as universally understood messages as the animation itself.

The visual gags and precisely timed action that we strove to perfect in crafting our Tom and Jerry cartoons would, we were convinced, appeal irresistibly to viewers throughout the world. In addition, I personally felt that Joe had drawn some of the cutest cartoon characters ever conceived on storyboards. Tom and Jerry were not only funny, they were lovable as well, and their indefatigable energy and dash gave the guys a charm that we felt put them in a league all of their own.

The variety of stories we came up with in this series provided excellent themes for the demonstration of these theories. One short that we did entitled *Fraidy Cat* provided about as vivid a display of visual personality animation and sight gags as any of the episodes we produced. The cartoon opens with our cat, Tom, shivering in delicious terror as he listens to the spine-tingling radio broadcast of a suspenseful ghost story. Jerry saunters out of his mouse hole, stops short when he spots Tom spellbound with fright, and breaks into a merry pantomime of mirthful amusement at the cat's gullibility. In addition to Jerry's silent, convulsive laughter, the little guy was animated in ways which had him pause at times in his guffaws, observe Tom's reactions of mounting terror to the broadcast, and lapse back into gleeful laughter. The tense, deliberate, and somewhat dimwitted reaction of fear by Tom to his ghost tale provided a nicely effective counterpoint to Jerry's quick and mischievously clever attitude.

Chemistry can occur in cartoons as surely as it does in live action movies. There is something magical about the way that characters can in their performances develop a spontaneous and often unpredictable charisma that goes beyond any calculated charm assigned to them as mere concepts.

Jerry was an incurable scene stealer. The little bastard just couldn't help it. Tom, as the antagonist, displays a pretty standard stock of expressions ranging from sly and sinister to outraged or terrified. Jerry, on the other hand, provided the pantomime wit of the shows, enacting a much greater variety of attitudes in which he could by turns be cunning, innocent, fearful, valiant, determined, impatient, mirthful, bewildered, and wise.

If Jerry provided much of the cleverness, however, Tom reliably came up with the essential menace and slapstick frustration. These traits combined to put the hallmark on Tom and Jerry's particular brand of cartoon humor.

The most enduring forms of humor, I believe, have an underlying element of poignancy beneath the hilarity. Beyond the standard gag fare of a cat-and-mouse chase theme, I believe viewers generally suspected that Tom and Jerry were "the best of enemies." There was a buddy system to their rivalry and no one ever seriously believed that Jerry was ever in mortal danger from Tom. Theirs was a private, joyful conflict. In extreme emergencies when either or both were threatened by a real villain, Tom and Jerry would team up and show a staunch loyalty to each other.

The unspoken law of the Tom and Jerry chases was that Jerry never picked on Tom first. Jerry's reactions were always a retaliation against Tom's attempts to nail him and he generally always came out on top. Thems was the rules of the game, and I've often thought that it would be nice if in this respect life imitated art.

The production system that Joe Barbera and I developed to turn out the Tom and Jerry cartoons in 1941 was a process that remained for the most part unchanged for the next sixteen years. After we developed our story, Joe would come up with the thumbnail sketches and I would time them. We would then give the artwork to the animators and in the process, I would often act out certain gags or facial expressions or body movements to give the animators as vivid a feel for the cartoon as possible. These dramatizations often carried over into the actual production of many of our cartoons in very spontaneous ways. And Tom and Jerry's various grunts, screeches, and exclamations for the most part were actually produced through the effusiveness of a loud and hammy Bill Hanna.

Most of the vocal sound effects we came up with for Tom and Jerry were recorded before the actual animation process began. Joe and I would schedule a session about every two months to record these vocal effects. Joe would be up in the booth along with the sound engineer, and would direct me as I did the vocals for Tom and occasionally Jerry. I would produce the appropriate screech or yowl called for in the cartoon and Joe would simply let me know if I needed to yell louder or longer.

I find it interesting to sometimes view these old cartoons just to hear a recording of what I sounded like as a young man screeching and yowling in his early thirties. Since both our cat and mouse were for the most part speechless, however, the soundtracks fail to provide any real record that I had also learned to speak by that time in my life!

In those days, we had what we would later regard as the luxury of a production schedule that allowed us enough time to refine through pencil tests whatever scenes in the cartoon we felt necessary to capture just the right expression on Tom or Jerry or any of the other characters and to hone the timing to perfection. Joe and I produced about a hundred and fifteen Tom and Jerry cartoons at MGM over a period of about seventeen years. That comes out to about six or seven shorts a year, and Joe and I are proud of the quality of every one of them, although neither one of us can honestly remember what the hell the gags and storylines were for each and every one of them.

During these early years of our partnership, Joe and I worked with a group of gifted animators who were to remain a part of our production unit for the next seventeen years at MGM. This team included five guys with whom I became very close friends: Irven Spence, Eddie Barge, Ken Muse, Ray Patterson, and Richard (Bick) Bickenbach. Irv Spence and I had gone to high school together, and even in those early days he had shown a remarkable flair for art work. Irv had drawn all of the cartoons for our high school senior album, and I can recall looking at those drawings and thinking that he was the greatest artist I had ever seen.

Shortly after joining Harman-Ising, I became convinced that Irv Spence should be working with us in the animation industry. When I first started to work for Hugh and Rudy, I had been absolutely amazed at all of the drawings that were involved in animation production and what a big part they played in making an animated cartoon. Irv and I had continued to keep in touch with each other following our graduation and I knew that he was working at a Standard Oil service station in Huntington Park, California.

One Friday afternoon I gave him a call and told him that I had something I wanted to bring down and show to him. I was anxious to bring Spence into the business, so I hit upon a bold plan. Friz Freleng was working with us as an animator. That evening, after the rest of the staff had gone home for the weekend, I sneaked over to Freleng's desk and swiped his drawings. Rushing this contraband down to Spence, I encouraged him to copy the drawings as a way of familiarizing himself with the kind of work we were doing, and then hustled back to the studio to replace the drawings before Friz walked in Monday morning.

My audacity was rewarded when Irv called me about three weeks later and elatedly informed me that he had gotten work at Winkler's Animation Studio. Upon showing some samples of his artwork to the management there he was hired on the spot and given work drawing the in-between illustrations for their cartoons. Spence was delighted to get away from that service station. He rose very quickly through the ranks to become a key animator at various studios including, Ub Iwerks Studio in Beverly Hills and Warner Bros. In 1940, Spence joined Joe and me at MGM and continued working with us on Tom and Jerry for nearly two decades.

Eddie Barge was another Harman-Ising alumnus. He was a very quiet guy, almost bashful, but a good animator. Eddie was probably a little better at animating Tom than Jerry, but he did a good job on either one and we were glad to have him on the show.

Ken Muse had joined us from the Disney studio. He was an extremely hardworking and prolific animator who turned out an amazing amount of cartoon footage. Kenny was very hard of hearing; because of his deafness, I think, he was somewhat shy. He didn't mix much socially with the rest of the group. He was totally absorbed in his work: He would even remain at his desk through morning and afternoon recesses and continue working on his drawings.

Bick Bickenbach was the fourth member of our team. I do not honestly recall if Bick came from the South, but he was in many ways the archetype of the Southern gentleman—courtly, God-fearing, and chivalrous. I had a tremendous fondness for Bick and regarded him as a great friend. One of Bickenbach's outstanding traits as an animator was his remarkable versatility. Bick could do character animation on either Tom or Jerry or on anything that we ever came up with.

Ray Patterson completed the unit. Ray was a former Disney alumnus and had worked on the animation of such features as *Dumbo* and *Fantasia*. Ray was a big, fun-loving guy who was generally easygoing; occasionally, though, he had a temper that would go off like a Roman candle. I learned a long time ago, however, that temper often goes along with talent. Ray's professional abilities were undeniably impressive, and he and Irv Spence did a lot in setting the tone for the personality animation of Tom and Jerry.

These men formed our key staff animators. After nearly fifty-five years of working in this business, I can still say with unalloyed conviction that those men made up one of the most gifted animation production teams I have ever known.

The relaxed production pace at MGM during those years provided us the opportunity to indulge in the experimentation and trial-and-error process that put a high gloss on those cartoons. It also allowed us to thoroughly enjoy ourselves in a work atmosphere that was almost entirely without stress and actually somewhat collegiate in its social environment. This camaraderie pervaded the whole studio, and I think most of us shared a general feeling of goodwill for the prospects of anyone working on Lot 2 regardless of what their job was.

I can recall occasional chats with one particularly ebullient office boy which eventually led me to make a pointed suggestion. "Jack," I remarked to him one morning, "maybe it's about time you quit running around in these halls as a gofer bringing coffee. You'd be a lot better off pushing your career on the sound stages." His name was Jack Nicholson, and I guess he took my advice!

The cartoon unit was almost entirely staffed by young people in their twenties or early thirties, and we were in general a high-spirited and occasionally mischievous bunch of kids. Very few of us, if any, were above pulling a practical joke or some prank on another susceptible coworker. Joe was a real Peck's Bad Boy at this, and still relates with glee incidents in which he placed water buckets on transoms that were rigged to drench an unsuspecting victim coming through the door.

Using the means at hand, we could also raise hell in other ways. Spitballs have always been a schoolroom staple of juvenile warfare, but in our offices we carried such assaults to a more lethal level. At some time or another some sinister prankster conceived the ingenious notion of using pushpins, generally employed for tacking up the storyboards, as darts aimed at the invitingly vulnerable feet of his fellow animators.

Pushpin fights spread like a barbed epidemic among the departments in our unit until cooler heads (and sore feet) prevailed to end this hazardous fad. Recalling those skirmishes now from the elevated wisdom of an eighty-six-year-old veteran, I can only marvel at our youthful stupidity—and wonder how we avoided making the eye patch a widely recognized professional badge of the animation business as dental bridgework might be in the National Hockey League.

There were other diversions as well, including occasional touch football games played on a large lawn located on the studio backlot. Joe has vivid recollections of producing stellar running plays in these contests. My memories of the games are somewhat hazier, but, consistent with the nature of our partnership, I would imagine that I generally participated as a referee.

Despite our close professional relationship at the studio, Joe Barbera and I seldom saw each other away from work. This was not due to any resentment or veiled hostility on either of our parts. I've always liked Joe and my admiration for his creative talents as an artist and singular gifts as a dynamic promoter and salesman of our shows is, I believe, one of the strongest bonds in our partnership.

In many ways, however, Joe Barbera and I are a classic study in contrasting personalities. Joe is a streetwise New Yorker with a stylish, self-assured flamboyance. He has an inveigling facility with persuasive dialogue and an unabashed love of creature comforts that would have drawn open approval from F. Scott Fitzgerald or any of the inspired sophisticates in his literature.

An author like Fitzgerald would have applauded Joe's panache, but I think I would have enjoyed a greater kinship with a writer like Zane Grey. I was born in New Mexico when that frontier was still a territory. As a native son of the West, I grew up with a passion for outdoor life that has included hiking, camping, fishing, and horseback riding. Joe, on the other hand, would not have been caught dead on a horse. He was infinitely more at home reclining by a fashionable resort's swimming pool than reeling in rainbows lakeside.

Joe and I have in general always spoken the same language in our mutual business concerns, but his words have always been delivered at a much greater velocity than my own. If they had ever been given the opportunity, Damon Runyon and Joe Barbera could have engaged in dazzling repartee, while someone like Gary Cooper and myself might have been able to thoroughly entertain ourselves with a cordial exchange of plainspoken laconisms.

But this is what makes horse races. Joe and I accepted and respected each other for our differences as much as our respective abilities, and neither of us sought to intrude on the other's preferred lifestyle. From the time that we first began working together, Joe and I have led completely different kinds of social lives. Joe has felt a strong affinity for Hollywood's celebrity society from the earliest years of our professional association. The glamorous parties and glittering social events in show business have always been a congenial environment for Joe, and his flair for cruising in these circles has won him many friendships with prominent folks in the motion picture and television industry.

My own friendships, in contrast, have principally been among animation colleagues. Many of the animators, layout artists, storyboard people, inkers, painters, and other individuals who put in their eight or nine—or twenty—hours a day working with me at the studio have become some of my best friends. Some have grown as close to me as family.

I have always considered myself extremely, perhaps extraordinarily, fortunate in the fact that my own family life as a child as well as my marriage and parenthood have been such happy experiences. The loving relationships my parents had for each other and with each of their children, I believe, was a kind of legacy that helped pave the way for the good marriage and home life that Vi and I have shared all these years.

Contrary to the old saw about in-laws being natural adversaries, one of my best friends for many years proved to be my brother-in-law, Leonard Gamble. We had grown up together and attended the same grammar school and high school. Leonard had married Vi's twin sister, Vera, shortly after Vi and I had wed. We formed a very close quartet and shared a great deal of our home life together. Our lifestyle, I imagine, when compared to a lot of other people in the entertainment business, was pretty tame.

We'd dine out, take in a movie, or maybe go for a drive. Hollywood nightclub or party circuits held no allure for any of us. If any show business columnist had ever decided to cover our comings and goings, they would have found us to be pretty disappointing copy. Without a doubt, the two most exciting events for Vi and myself during those first years of our marriage were the births of our two children, David and Bonnie.

David was born on January 3, 1939, and Bonnie three years later on January 27, 1942. By the time our kids came along, we had acquired our own home. I had signed a contract with MGM that paid me a princely salary of $175 a week along with options, and I felt reasonably confident that Joe and I were turning out winning cartoons that would enable us to continue working for MGM indefinitely. About a year after joining MGM, Vi and I decided to purchase a piece of property in the heart of the San Fernando Valley that consisted of a five-acre plot of walnut trees. We were originally going to build out there, but once we began to go out and visit the place, we discovered that it was too far from my work in Culver City.

We decided to trade that property for a lot in Sherman Oaks. It was a nice site set in a secluded fold of hills and located close enough to work so I would be able to drive to the studio in about thirty minutes. That is where Vi and I built our first home. I remember how excited we were on the day construction was completed. To celebrate moving into our new home, I suggested to Vi that we treat ourselves to a special dinner at Eaton's Chicken House on Ventura Boulevard. Like two kids on a first date we seated ourselves at a table and ordered our meal. With a flourish, I produced a white candle I had brought with me from work and we shared a candle-lit dinner to commemorate the housewarming of a home we have owned and lived in for over fifty years.

It was a good life. Vi and I were happy together with our two kids. We were both devout Catholics and felt abundantly blessed by God for having a home, a family, and a job which to me was a well-spring of creative adventure and just plain fun.

This did not mean that we enjoyed an entirely idyllic existence, however. During the early years of our family life, we faced what is undoubtedly the worst kind of crisis that can arise for any parents: The critical illnesses suffered by their children.

Our daughter Bonnie suffered throughout her childhood from a kidney condition that at times was an unrelenting source of agony. Here was a little kid who often had to endure the kind of pain that would have reduced an adult to tears. She had to undergo several operations in an attempt to alleviate the severe cramps and other grievous symptoms inflicted by hydro-nephrosis, which she has continued to valiantly battle as an adult.

The trauma and despair of Bonnie's illness had a permanent and profound effect on all of us, and both my son David and I have over the years continued to contribute funds in support of the foundation that researches the illness.

There was one other real crisis that we faced as a family during those early years. Our son David fell critically ill with rheumatic fever when he was about four years old. The real dread of the disease is the grave damage this illness can inflict on a victim's heart. Our physician prescribed complete bed rest for the boy and offered us the hopeful prediction of a complete recovery providing we followed a strict convalescence program that restricted all physical activity.

David was confined to a crib three feet wide and five feet long that was elevated about thirty inches off the floor. That became his home for the next nine months as we prayerfully attempted to nurse him back to health. Violet maintained a devoted vigil over our son that I am convinced was entirely responsible for his eventual full recovery.

I can still remember her preparing a breakfast of cereal, scrambled eggs, and fresh fruit for him every weekday as I prepared to go to work. My voice would sometimes catch a little as I waved goodbye to him in the morning. "We'll work some puzzles tonight, David," I'd promise. David always had a smile like a sunbeam. His whole face would light up in response and he'd answer with something like, "The one with the purple pirate, Dad!" Besides looking a little flushed and maybe a little thin, he seemed to be fine. "Jesus!" I'd think to myself, "How could our son be sick?" The idea of our robust little boy facing life as an invalid seemed outrageously obscene.

With Vi's diligent care and our loving encouragement, David rallied. After many anxious months of doing all we could think of to nurture him through his sickness and confinement, the doctor one day delivered the thrilling pronouncement that our son was healthy and that his heart was perfectly sound.

When I was a child and our family had gone through difficult times, we had often been counseled by my mother with the plain-spoken admonition to buck up and count our blessings. Mother's advice came back to me clear as a bell the day my wife and I were able to send our son outside to play. In that moment of gratitude, however, I found the blessings we'd received too numerous to count.

Another crisis had passed, and our cup had "runneth over." Despite our prosperous comfort, however, we knew all too well that everyone in the country in 1943 was living in times of intense turmoil. World War II overshadowed all of our lives. At about this time, Rudy Ising returned to MGM—only this time he was in uniform. Rudy had been commissioned a Major in the Army Air Corps Intelligence and was assigned to supervise the production of animated military training films.

The war department had quite sensibly reasoned that it would be a lot less expensive to produce these pictures in animated form rather than as live action films. By employing our animators and artists to come up with the required illustrations and movements for these films at the studio, many of the logistics of staff and crew recruitment, transportation, location shooting, and the other complexities that would otherwise be both expensive and a general pain in the ass if they were filmed in live action were circumvented. Cartoons were a lot cheaper and a lot less trouble to produce, and with the right technical narration they could be as precisely graphic and instructional as necessary for training films.

When Fred Quimby phoned our office and notified Joe and me that we would be working with Rudy on the training films, I was frankly a little apprehensive over the reunion. Could it be that Rudy was a little sore at me for deciding to leave the Harman-Ising Studio a few years back in favor of working at MGM? There had been a lot of competitive activity among the various production units in those early days, including Rudy's and Joe's and mine in all of our attempts to develop the successful cartoon series that would put Quimby's studio on the map. All of that made me wonder if feelings might be a little strained between us.

All of this tension evaporated the moment Rudy walked through the door. Ising cut an impressive figure in uniform that contrasted vividly from the informal guy in shirt-sleeves who had been my boss at Harman-Ising. The gold leaves of his major's insignia appeared to add a singular gleam to his shoulders, and the immaculate tailoring of that uniform seemed to rival even that of the dapper Joe Barbera in elegance.

Aside from his martial splendor, Rudy seemed as leisurely warm and unpretentious a guy as ever. There wasn't the remotest suggestion of any hard feelings regarding the divergent paths our careers had recently taken, and he seemed eager for us to begin working as a team on the training films. Rudy, Joe, and myself devised an efficient team operation that worked very well during a collaboration which lasted for the duration of the war effort.

Rudy would bring in a rough storyboard of the proposed cartoon that had been supplied to him by the Signal Corps. These boards were based upon a variety of military tactical themes including films on sanitation, submarine camouflage operations, and destroyer attack procedures for the United States Navy. The three of us would go over the storyboards in several meetings and discuss the development of the film. From that point, under Rudy's supervision, Joe and I would carry on with the production process in the same manner as if we were turning out any other cartoon. Joe would refine the storyboards and I would proceed with the timing and direction of the animation.

The production time involved in these projects would vary according to the theme and the complexity of the subject involved. For example, some of the films we did on sanitation which provided instruction on such straightforward subjects as efficient latrine installation or the purification of drinking water required as little as four to six weeks to complete. This was in marked contrast to the complexities of producing a vital film on the how to coordinate the movements of several destroyers to provide a smoke screen camouflage for the concealment of battleships.

Every military project was given top priority by our studio. If Rudy suddenly appeared and presented a new storyboard to us in the midst of any of our other production activity, the work was immediately set aside until the current production demands for the military had been met. Both Joe and I undertook this work with earnest commitment. Utilizing our skills to produce these training films allowed us an opportunity to make a contribution to the war effort in a way that a lot of other people couldn't, and we were grateful that our services could be of value. I don't think I ever really doubted that we'd win the war, but I knew damn well that we needed to do everything we could to make sure that we didn't *lose* it as well.

Completion of the service training films marked the end of my professional collaboration with Rudy Ising. Regretfully, I never had an opportunity to work again with either of my former mentors who gave me that first job at Harman-Ising Studios. Both Hugh Harman and Rudy Ising continued to free-lance in the business as animators after leaving MGM, but it is their glory days as young and vital producers of classic Looney Tunes and Merrie Melodies cartoons that will ensure them lasting esteem as pioneers of motion picture animation. Hugh Harman passed away at an early age, and I felt a tremendous sadness upon hearing of his death.

Happily, Rudy Ising and I were able to enjoy a warm, if often long-distance, friendship with each other through mail and telephone correspondence until Rudy's death a few years ago. My memories of the months Joe and I spent working with Major Rudolph Ising in contributing to the war effort are as cherished as any other I recall during those early years at MGM. We were friends, comrades, and confidants, all working together for a greater good that hopefully brought the best out in all of us through artistic expression. Serving with Rudy was more than a duty for me, just as much as working with Joe and our crew has always been more than a job.

Through the years, I've talked to a number of people who seem to feel that job friendships are limited in their depth by the fact that they extend only to working together. Perhaps they feel this way because they find their own jobs uncongenial and discern their friendships by whom they are willing to share their leisure time. But I have never really felt that way. Part of friendship is sharing good times with people, and many of the best times in my life were enjoyed at work. The affection people have for each other and the affection they all share for the work they do and the things they create are bonds that are strong and true.

There is an old Celtic blessing that goes: "May the worst day of your future be no more sorrowful than the best day of your past." That is an Irishman's sentiment, and my family and a lot of the people I work with will probably tell you that I am incurably sentimental. At this time of my life, I'm pretty much getting on in age. Still, there is one small wonder inside me that has never really grown up. It is a kind of wistfulness for the future as well as the past—and a love for the "good new days" that come with every morning.

Chapter Five

Leading Roles

Carpools are an old and honored institution that fortunately continue to be encouraged in today's energy-conscious society. Ride-sharing to work during World War II was an earnest civilian attempt to conserve gas rations and assist with the national war effort. There were several people working at MGM living in the San Fernando Valley at the time, and a few of my neighbors and I decided to make the daily trip together across the Santa Monica Mountains to work.

Since we had to contend with a shortage of automobiles among our group as well as gasoline rationing, the ridesharing plan was doubly practical. Of the handful of folks who joined our little carpool unit every day, only Tex Avery and I owned cars. Tex and I agreed to shift off every other week driving to work, and every morning one of us set out and picked up the other and made the rounds collecting passengers: a young writer named Rick Hogan, a couple of neighboring animators, and a young woman named Edna Pidgeon. Edna was the daughter of actor Walter Pidgeon and worked as an animation checker at the studio. She was a bright gal who, along with three or four other artists, was responsible for the quality control end of cartoon production, such as reviewing the animation to insure that the characters were "on model," or properly drawn.

I owned a black Pontiac sedan at the time and on my week I'd swing by Tex's house around seven-thirty in the morning. By eight, we had picked up the rest of the gang and were on our way. Our route to work never varied. There were no freeways flanking the mountains out of the San Fernando Valley to Los Angeles in those days. We never missed them, for the two-lane road that we took was a lot more scenic with a lot less traffic. We would turn south onto Beverly Glen off Ventura Boulevard and head over the Santa Monica Mountains and over Mulholland Drive on a woodsy, almost rural cruise that took us directly into Beverly Hills.

This was always the highlight of our trip, and I don't think we ever tired of gawking. Bus tours through Beverly Hills and purchasing maps to the stars' homes may be a standard tourist attraction today. For a carload of kids working at jobs making cartoons during the 1940s, the chance to motor past a kingdom of stately mansions in this opulent neighborhood was just as intriguing a tour and never lost its novelty.

Continuing south to Pico Boulevard, we turned right and headed west to a wide road called Overland Avenue which brought us over a steep hill and right down into Culver City and the MGM studio. Our carpool excursions lasted until the end of the war and are among my most pleasant memories of that time in my life. Those daily thirty-minute drives to and from work were invariably enlivened with bawdy humor and hilarity. Although Edna was the only woman among us, she was a good sport about all the on-key, off-color kidding and could be as unblushingly crazy as the rest of us.

Any ride with Tex Avery, of course, was a cinch to be one of side-splitting hysteria. Tex's backseat humor was as spontaneously zany as any of his wildest cartoons and often a lot racier. Tex exerted a tremendous professional influence over my career in animation. He was looked up to by just about everyone in the industry as an exceptionally gifted animator and director. Although he was only a few years older than me, he had already established himself as a kind of prodigy in our business with his distinctive style of exaggerated timing and direction of frenetic madcap Merrie Melodies cartoons at Warners. Like a lot of other pioneers in the cartoon business, Tex Avery remained a kind of unsung hero in our business for many years to just about everyone except his colleagues. But to me, he is one of the greatest personalities in cartoon history.

I admired Avery for his phenomenal sense of timing along with his imaginative flair for wild gags. They combined to make his cartoons among the funniest ever produced in the business. Whenever time permitted, I would take the opportunity to run one of Avery's latest cartoons and study it on the movieola, frame by frame, in order to hone my own skills in timing.

Tex produced a variety of wonderful cartoons at MGM including the popular Droopy series and a short cartoon called *The Blitz Wolf* which won an Academy Award in 1942. For some reason we seemed to exude a strange kind of cartoon karma at MGM that brought a great turnover of talent at the place, and Tex was one of the few directors who remained at Metro-Goldwyn-Mayer with Joe and myself throughout the many professional vicissitudes of the cartoon studio. Tex and I formed a very close friendship during those years. We shared some rollicking good times together on fishing and camping trips at a time in our careers which were nearly as freewheeling and unpredictable as any of Avery's most outrageous cartoon creations.

By 1943, I had been in the animation business for about thirteen years. I recall my amazement over the impressive creative and technical advances that had been achieved in cartoon production during that relatively short period of time. Animation had come a long way since the rudimentary black-and-white Looney Tunes and Merrie Melodies that I had been weaned upon as an apprentice at Harman-Ising Studio. Aside from the addition of color, the cartoons being produced by Disney, Warner Bros., MGM, and other studios during the early 1940s had attained a new sophistication and elan in personality animation and story writing.

Watching the results of our production efforts projected on the big screen never ceased to be a somewhat astonishing experience for me. This was the grand vision that had captivated me as a kid. It still seemed incredible to me as an adult to witness how such broad and exuberant cinematic fantasies sprang from the methodical yet arcane processes of ninety artists and animators working together in the prosaic environment of sequestered little offices littered with pencil sketches.

Somewhere in the process of watching that seven-minute run of film called a cartoon, a curious phenomenon often occurs in the mind of a viewer called the suspension of disbelief. At that moment, illusion becomes reality—an animated reality—and the images we see take on a dimension of magical credibility. A really good cartoon becomes a thing of make-believe in the sense that it somehow magically compels us *to believe* and live the fantasy we see.

Joe and I were always striving to enhance this phenomenon in our animation, but even we were somewhat taken aback when Gene Kelly showed up at our office one morning in 1943 and proposed that we test the boundaries even further in a novel way. Gene was about thirty-two years old at the time and was already a major talent at MGM. Unknown to his adoring audience, Kelly possessed an intense drive and single-minded determination for creative control of his career and movies that belied the smiling Irishman's image by which he was so well known.

When Gene walked into our office, it was apparent that he was brimming with a creative enthusiasm about something. "Bill! Joe!" was the opener delivered with a grin and an Irish lilt. "Gotta way to make your little mouse Jerry into a star!"

Joe and I glanced at each other a bit nonplussed. "But he already is a star, Gene," I pointed out. Gene blinked at this and his grin widened. "I mean a bigger star alongside of *me!*" he declared.

It turned out that Kelly was in a huge excitement over the idea of doing a dance routine with a cartoon character for an upcoming MGM feature called *Anchors Aweigh*. Gene had gotten the idea from an assistant choreographer named Stanley Donen (who later, of course, became an award-winning director in his own right) and had gone to Disney to propose that he do the dance with Mickey Mouse.

When Disney declined the offer, Kelly, undaunted, decided to shift his sights to another up-and-coming animation star. He appealed to Fred Quimby to let him dance with our own Jerry Mouse. It proved to be a hard sell. Quimby turned him down flat. Persistent as ever, Gene went over or rather "under" Quimby's head and pitched the concept to Joe and me.

I personally thought it was a great idea. Including animation figures in live-action sequences had been done in a limited form in the past, but here was a chance to combine the two mediums in a really sparkling and spectacular way. Joe expressed similar enthusiasm over the project, but Quimby was our boss. It was up to him.

Gene had the tenacity of a fighting Irishman, but even more importantly, he carried the formidable clout of being one of the most powerful stars at MGM. Undismayed by Quimby's refusal, Kelly related his wishes directly to Louis B. Mayer. In short order, Joe and I found ourselves assigned to work with Gene on the animation sequence of the film.

The process of combining live action and animation in a single film proved to be a challenging and involved undertaking. Since the precise animation of Jerry's movements depended upon the dance number choreographed by Gene Kelly, we needed to obtain a copy of the entire film sequence of Kelly's dance routine. The segment of Gene dancing by himself on the set was then filmed. A rough storyboard was drawn depicting Kelly's dance routine with our mouse, Jerry.

During the shooting, either Joe or I would be on the set to assist Gene if necessary to make the right eye contact or movements necessary to make it appear as if he were dancing with Jerry. Gene was photographed doing his whole routine dancing into the foreground with the camera trucking back, all of the time keeping his eye where Jerry would eventually be. The dance came to a stop and Gene went into his final pose.

Using the film of Kelly's dancing as a guide, we proceeded to animate Jerry so that we could either match his movements with Kelly's or draw his actions in whatever way was necessary to accommodate the routine. By taking that film frame by frame, we were able to blow it up to our working size of a twelve-inch field and animate Jerry, matching him to the live-action filmed sequence of Gene.

Once this had been done, a test reel of the preliminary pencil animation was processed with Gene's filmed sequence to make a work print that was viewed by Kelly and ourselves to make sure that everything was synchronized as it was supposed to be. After Kelly had approved the test, the pencil drawings were then inked, painted, and photographed, and then superimposed on the live-action film.

The story situation worked up for Jerry's role in the film called for him to appear as the forlorn little ruler of a mythical kingdom. Kelly was cast as a jaunty, wandering sailor. Upon learning from King Jerry that he "just hadda" forbid music in his kingdom because the king himself did not know how to dance, he proceeds to teach Jerry how to hoof it in a marvelous cavort around the throne room. The resulting four-minute sequence turned out to be a very nice debut for Jerry Mouse in his first speaking film role. To my relief, Jerry proved to be very easy to work with on this project and was, as usual, very cooperative, professional, and prompt. Most important, perhaps, he did not let this stardom go to his head and make unreasonable salary demands to his bosses.

Our cat, Tom, was given a relatively minor role. Actually, it was only a walk-on that featured him as a servant in attendance to King Jerry. Tom seemed a little disgruntled over this and I think he kind of took it out on Jerry in the next regular cat-and-mouse chase cartoon that they did together.

Gene Kelly deserved, I believe, every kudo he received for that feature. His dance routine with Jerry proved to be an exhilarating display of brilliant choreography and razor-sharp direction that complemented our animation to perfection. The sequence turned out to be the highlight of the movie, and its popular success encouraged the hope in both Joe and me that we would be able to work on other combined live-action/animation projects.

Apparently, George Sidney, who directed *Anchors Aweigh* (1945), shared our enthusiasm. One year after that film's release, George cut a deal with us to provide an animation sequence for the opening credits of another MGM feature called *Holiday in Mexico (1946)*. In 1953, our cat Tom was also given a chance to get his paws wet—along with every other part of him—with Jerry and actress Esther Williams in an animated underwater ballet segment for the film *Dangerous When Wet*.

The most elaborate undertaking in this genre, however, involved a reunion with Gene Kelly on the production of the film *Invitation to the Dance*. Unlike previous features, neither Tom nor Jerry appeared in the film. The script called for a lengthy segment titled "Sinbad the Sailor" which has Kelly acquiring a lamp with a genie in Bagdhad and embarking on a series of Arabian Nights adventures in a completely animated world.

By utilizing a production process similar to that employed in *Anchors Aweigh*, we were able to convincingly create such intriguing illusions as those of Gene dancing with an animated harem girl and a choreographed confrontation with an undulating serpent whose movement matched Kelly's intricate dance moves.

Unfortunately, *Invitation to the Dance* never enjoyed the popular audience reception that made *Anchors Aweigh* a hit film nine years earlier. A big part of this was probably due to the fact that the presentation of the movie's storylines was done entirely in dance performances and without dialogue. Kelly had directed the film and set a new artistic precedent in moviemaking, but the treatment proved to be too unconventional for audiences at the time.

Despite this disappointment, I derived great personal satisfaction from the aesthetic appeal and charm of the film's animation segment. The blissful waltz of Gene with his harem sweetheart and their fanciful courtship among a cascade of falling leaves and sublime painted backgrounds were beautifully animated and imparted the film with a classic romance that was as graceful in imagery as any of the Disney productions that were then being released.

The growing sophistication of these combined live-action/animated features showcased the ascendance of cartoonmaking as a progressive art form that was proving itself as commercially vital as any other aspect of the entertainment industry. Dollar for dollar, the return profit earned by the money invested by our studio into each Tom and Jerry cartoon returned a greater revenue than that of any major motion picture MGM ever produced.

The popular appeal of Tom and Jerry generated one of the largest and most loyal audiences of major cartoon personalities in the world. Fred Quimby's office displayed ample evidence of this fact with a glittering display of seven Oscars on his desk that he eventually acquired as our animated series was elected several times the best cartoon of the year. The first Academy Award came in 1943, for *Yankee Doodle Mouse*.

Joe and I had watched this collection grow over a period of several years and had pretty much contented ourselves with the knowledge that our cartoons had earned such consistent acclaim. The annual Academy Awards ceremonies evoked as much excitement among those of us in animation as anyone else working in the entertainment industry. There was a mystique to the Oscar from its conception in 1927, when the Academy was founded. The first awards ceremony was held in 1929, but it was not until 1932 that the Academy of Motion Picture Arts and Sciences recognized animated cartoons as productions worthy of receiving such prestigious awards.

It was a strict policy of the Academy to award Oscars to the producers of the winning cartoons. The Academy excluded anyone else who had been creatively involved with the production of the cartoon from accepting the award in the ceremony. Since Fred Quimby's name appeared as producer and Joe and I were credited only as directors, Fred was designated the award recipient even though he had never been creatively involved in the production of our cartoons.

During the early years, neither Joe nor I ever attended the award ceremonies, primarily because neither one of us owned a tuxedo at the time. Our adoration of Oscar had always been from afar, and we had generally learned the outcome of the awards by reading the announcements of the winners in the trade papers the next morning.

One afternoon, however, we decided to hatch a little scheme calculated to net us a little souvenir of our professional association with Quimby's seven golden statuettes. The word spread quickly that day in our unit that Fred Quimby had been called to a meeting on the main lot—leaving his office invitingly unattended. Acting with an opportunistic swiftness that would have made Jerry Mouse proud, Joe and I marshaled our little group of animators: Irv Spence, Kenny Muse, Eddie Barge, Dick Bickenbach, and, of course, Joe and myself. A few minutes later, a half dozen of us assembled around Fred's desk, grinning in conspiratorial pride as a photograph was snapped with seven little Oscars all in a row before us.

Academy Awards and screen credits notwithstanding, none of those alluring prestige symbols ever caused much commotion at home. As far as my two kids, David and Bonnie, were concerned, their dad simply headed for the office every day like any other father and came home every evening after work. David and Bonnie enjoyed watching cartoons as much as any children, but they were generally pretty "underwhelmed" over the fact that their dad produced them for a living.

Part of this was, I imagine, due to the probability that most kids at a very young age seem to accept cartoons at face value as natural enchantments that have very little to do with the eight-hour mechanics involving the kind of systematic production that turned out mixmasters and Studebaker cars. Cartoons for young children simply "happen" and are enjoyed for their own emotional appeal, without any burdensome regard for their origin or development.

As very young children, probably neither of my kids gave much thought to relating what I did for a living to what they saw on the big screen in theatres with their friends at a Saturday matinee. They loved the 'toon—seven minutes of colorful images of fun and fantasy—but displayed little curiosity about the process that brought about their existence. This was fine with me. After all, cartoons are part of the experience of a child's wonder years. Neither Vi nor I were in any hurry to have our kids discover that there was no Santa Claus, or dissipate the magic of cartoons by emphasizing to them, during their ephemeral years of make-believe, the mechanics of their creation.

The occupations that I and a couple of my neighbors in Sherman Oaks worked at were good examples of how influential the entertainment industry was in providing jobs for young people in Southern California at the time. My neighbor on the left was a guy named Ed Snyder who worked at 20th-Century Fox as a cameraman. The neighbor on the right was a fellow named Jim Christie, who was employed as a publicist at Universal Studio.

So every morning all of us pulled out of our respective driveways for work. Ed headed for 20th-Century Fox, Jim to Universal, and I motored my way to MGM. None of us attached any particular glamour to our jobs, although I believe we were all eager to become as successful as possible at what we did.

Both David and Bonnie enjoyed cartoons as much as any children, but their childhood preceded the birth of that happy pajama ritual called "Saturday Morning Cartoon Shows" by about a decade. Characters like Huckleberry Hound and Yogi Bear were still unborn concepts, along with the baby boom TV generation that became their premier audience.

The only time I can actually remember either of our kids enjoying anything close to such a program experience occurred one morning when I received a call at work from my daughter's school. Bonnie was having a particularly tough day because of the kidney condition that never ceased to plague her, and the school nurse decided that morning that it would be best that she be sent home. For some reason, Violet was away from home when the school called the house, so the school phoned me at the studio and asked if I could pick up my daughter.

We had a prescription to help treat Bonnie's medical condition, but what was I going to do about helping to ease the boredom of a little girl who would suddenly be transplanted from a friendly classroom to her dad's alien work environment? The only thing that I could think of was to drive my daughter to the studio and figure out something when I got there. Leaving her schoolbooks in the car, Bonnie was permitted a happy respite from her homework and spent a thoroughly delightful afternoon in one of the MGM projection rooms watching Tom and Jerry cartoons.

Because Boy Scouting had been such an enjoyable experience in my own youth, I was pleased when my son became involved in scouting. He pretty much followed his own head in this decision, but I was glad that we would share a common ground in our attempts at mastering all of the woodcraft, knot-tying, and campfire lore that made being a kid such a wholesome adventure for me. But more importantly, I was happy to share a basic code with my son that spoke from a creed beyond the arbitrary dictatorship of being a parent. The Scout oath was, in my eyes, a kind of bond between parents and their kids. In many ways, it was an equalizing pledge that challenged any generation to simply individually do the very best they could and to respect each other.

My own enthusiasm for the Boy Scouts, along with a keen desire to share some father-and-son activities with David, prompted me to become a scoutmaster. The experience was as rewarding for me as it was for any of the boys.

We had twelve scouts in Troop 2, and they were all good kids. The weekly meetings we held provided sessions of quality time in guidance, communication, and activity planning that were all geared towards encouraging and promoting wholesome life choices for the boys. Our scouting activities were for the most part community endeavors involving parents and teachers. It was a committed comradeship which proved to have enduring merit, many of those kids in my troop, including David, went on to make good lives and careers for themselves.

Over the years I've endeavored to maintain a supportive relationship with the Boy Scouts of America through both financial sponsorship and as a kind of goodwill ambassador for the organization. As one of our neighborhood's favorite den mothers, Violet shared my devotion to scouting.

While we're on the subject of scouting, I'll own up to a little admission. As proud and grateful as Vi and I are for the wonderful awards, including the later Emmys, that have come our way during all of these years in the cartoon business, one of our most cherished honors is the Americanism Award that was presented to me in 1991 by the Great Western Council of the Boy Scouts of America. Mother and Dad would have been proud.

Both Vi and I considered it a rare blessing that family history seemed to repeat itself in the sense that David and Bonnie turned out from early on to be the best of pals. David was always very protective of his kid sister and although I think part of this solicitude was probably due to Bonnie's delicate health, he nevertheless genuinely enjoyed his sister's company and conversation.

I imagine that most parents can probably identify with the mingled emotions of amazement, intrigue, and pride that Violet and I felt over seeing how the emerging personalities of our kids seemed to mirror so many of our own character traits. Children in many ways provide echoes and reflections of our own youth and past. We see them making many of the same mistakes we made and trying to cover them in the same ways.

We see and feel them go through the same self-conscious struggles, the tenuous knee-bruising attempts at balance in learning to ride a two-wheeler, or remaining upright on a pair of roller skates, and all the awkwardness and the achievements involved in the childhood rituals of becoming an okay individual. Once in a while, you'll catch a turn of the head, a note in the voice, or a sparkle in the eye that makes you think you're standing behind yourself—with a strange new glimmer of understanding that brings you poignantly closer in spirit to your own parents.

Bonnie had inherited a lot of her dad's own basic shyness that seemed at times to conflict with an instinctive need to assert herself. I always felt a particularly deep affinity for my daughter because of this and always will. David, as a youngster, displayed ample evidence of possessing a spirit every bit as gregarious and open-hearted as his mother's. From a very early age, David had an optimistic self-confidence that always seemed to draw a happy following of neighborhood buddies.

If much of this recounting sounds a lot like apple pie and Old Glory, it is also pretty much true to what our world was like during the

1950s. Admittedly, it was a less complex time than what we know today, but it was not, as cultural sentimentalists might suggest, an idyllic era. We had our fears of atom bombs, gang violence, crime, unemployment, and of having our children fall prey to such sorrows as alcoholism, juvenile delinquency, and drug abuse. Above all, we had concerns as well as hopes for the future. Regardless of the times in which any generation lives, "tomorrow" will always be the unknown realm that humbles us all and reminds of our perpetual innocence and vulnerability.

Vi and I both knew that life could be hard. After all, we'd spent our youth in the worst economic depression the country had ever known. We'd gone through a war. We read the newspapers. Our participation in such community activities as scouting was an effort to prepare our kids for life's difficulties and challenges rather than a mere ritual of living some abstract ideal of the American Dream.

One of the most enjoyable aspects of our family life in the San Fernando Valley was the fact that my parents lived only a few miles away from our home. Dad and I had built the house together while I was still working at Harman-Ising Studio and our households had over the years virtually merged into a single close-knit family unit. Time had touched both my parents lightly. Their mutual enthusiasm for living was perennially youthful and I found my relationship with them was about as confidingly reassuring as it had been when I was a child. My father still called me "Brother" just as he had when I was a boy, and Mother was as formidably solicitous as ever over her only son's welfare.

As a young husband and the father of two young kids of my own, I pretty much felt that I had entered the prime of my life and still reveled in the entertainment of youthful prospects. In many respects, I didn't feel that I'd changed much from the skinny kid who had emptied wastebaskets at Hugh and Rudy's studio twenty-three years earlier. The only noteworthy sign of advancing age seemed to be a marked graying at the temples in my hair. This minor transformation was something that I generally paid little attention to beyond the time it took to shave in the morning.

One afternoon however, a little pearl of candor uttered from the mouth of a babe changed my whole perspective in the matter of gray hair. Driving home from the studio one day, I happened to see two little kids working a lemonade stand they had set up on their front lawn. This touched a tender spot in my heart, for our own kids had both been fond of operating a similar neighborhood enterprise.

Pulling the car over, I got out and paid my ten cents to sample their product. The kids eyed me expectantly. "Well," ventured one after a moment's hesitation, "how do you like it, mister?" I drained the glass and returned it to them. "Not bad," I assessed. "Not bad at all. Pretty good, in fact." The kids brightened perceptibly at this approval.

"So, how's business?" I asked as I got ready to hit the road again.

"It's been pretty good today," responded one kid with a lingering look at my hair. "There was another old man who stopped by earlier today and bought some lemonade from us, too."

There it was. I was getting on. I must have just rounded the corner into forty at the time. I drove home in a thoughtful reverie. Pulling the car into our driveway, I got out and walked into a kitchen fragrant with Vi's good cooking. "Honey," I informed her with a rueful tone in my voice, "You're married to an old man!"

I was indeed becoming prematurely gray, but it was genetics, not the animation industry that was starting to turn my hair white. Not at all! No, the cartoon business had been good to me. It had buffered both my family and myself from the harsh stringencies of the Depression, helped buy us a home, provided us with respectable savings, and seemed to promise a secure future in an occupation that had become to me a kind of magnificent obsession.

Metro-Goldwyn-Mayer Studio had become a professional home to both Joe Barbera and myself and I think we felt pretty secure that Bill and Joe and Tom and Jerry would continue on as a winning combination for as long as cats naturally chased mice and the MGM lion continued to roar his benediction over the opening credits of our cartoons. It had been a good run and it looked like it was going to get even better. This would certainly prove to be true for a few more years.

As corny as it may sound, I was so enduringly enthralled with my work that I can recall repeatedly asking myself for years the same question at the beginning of each work day as I said my good mornings to people and headed to the office I shared with Joe. The question never varied in wording and I never really bothered to ponder the answer. "How much luckier," I would wonder happily to myself, "can we get?" Then one day, as the gray hair and undiminished optimism continued to thrive for Bill Hanna and his ever youthful dark-haired partner, Joe Barbera, the lion stopped roaring for us.

Chapter Six

Leap of Fate

I've always found the catch phrase "cartoon classics" to be nearly as amusing as the concept of cartoons themselves. The truth of the matter is that theatrical cartoons during the earliest years were generally regarded by film audiences as anything but classic entertainment. Cartoons were the animated versions of the funny papers, mere warm-up acts that led to the main event of the live action motion picture.

In 1938 this perspective changed dramatically, of course, with the stunning popular success of Walt Disney's animated feature *Snow White and the Seven Dwarfs*. I had read about the development of the film for months in the trade papers and eagerly anticipated the picture's release.

Snow White and the Seven Dwarfs premiered in December 1937, and during 1937 and 1938 earned an estimated eight million dollars, a phenomenal amount of money for that time. *Snow White* was, in fact, one of the original theatrical blockbuster hits. According to estimates of box office receipts, the picture captured a greater audience on its initial release than the spectacular hit *Star Wars*.

I was living in an apartment on Olympic Boulevard at the time that was located just a block or so from the Carthay Circle Theatre, where the movie premiered. I can recall standing on the sidelines watching the throngs of formally attired young people who had been involved in the movie's production marching into the glittering theatre house as spotlights swept the sky.

About a week later on payday, I walked back down to that theatre, eagerly bought my ticket and spent the next two hours or so enjoying one of the most memorable viewing experiences of my life. I was absolutely mesmerized by the faultless grace of Disney's animation. The film was an unalloyed masterpiece, an archetype that revealed to me perhaps for the first time in my life the awesome potential of the industry with which I had chosen to ally myself.

A pioneer in my mind has always been someone who simply got somewhere or did something first. There is a good deal of luck involved in being primary in a certain field, but I think there is a certain amount of vision required in the process as well. Walt Disney's *Snow White* has always been for me the visionary work of the premier pioneer of theatrical animation. Disney's filmmaking feat helped open my eyes to the possibility that a greater destiny than I'd ever imagined awaited the heretofore humble cartoon.

Beyond the sheer fun that Joe and I got out of producing our Tom and Jerry cartoons, I derived a special satisfaction from the challenge of trying to impart our cartoons with their own hallmark of animation excellence. This meant to me, in particular, a constant striving to hone my instincts for innovative timing in the musical scoring and direction of the cartoon. The quality of timing can either invest a picture with the vital rhythm needed to bring its characters kicking and screaming into the viewer's world or produce a stillborn cartoon that appears flat, mechanical, and contrived. Despite all the laughs we hoped to generate on the screen, and the hilarity we often enjoyed around the storyboards, producing cartoons in many ways is a serious, if not always sober, business.

The aesthetic excellence of the Disney theatrical features and the growing audience loyally commanded by the always reliable seven-minute cartoon shorts had helped stir within me the realization of—dare I say—a new sense of *dignity* to the cartoon business as a legitimate industry with great exciting commercial potential. Admittedly, production processes had fundamentally remained the same since the early Silly Symphonies and Looney Tunes days. The growing sophistication of the animation itself, resulting from the ingenious skills of the artists in our business, however, began to convince me that cartoons had come of age.

A lot of film had gone through movieolas since Disney ushered Mickey Mouse into sound motion pictures in *Steamboat Willie* in 1928. Each flicker and frame of all that footage had helped evolve the cartoon from a mere whimsical novelty to a cultural product of alluring artistry. Anyone viewing a reel of an old Bosko or Krazy Kat short today would undoubtedly regard them as pretty primitive fare compared to the Bugs Bunny or Tom and Jerry cartoons that appeared a mere decade later.

Figuratively speaking, the contrast between them was as distinct as black and white. Literally speaking, this was also true, for the introduction of color to film in the late 1930s produced what was undoubtedly the most dramatic visual enhancement to cartoons. With regard to the quality of the animation itself, however, I believe that the primary element that helped give cartoon characters such a credible feel in their look and movements was the refinement of the directorial timing of the pictures.

Timing a cartoon in many respects is similar to orchestrating a musical arrangement. It involves the alignment of visual images with precisely coordinated rhythms that are calculated to impart a sense of emotion and energy to the animated drawings. This was a particularly critical process when it involved the introduction of sound to cartoons.

By using the precise beat of the ever-reliable metronome as an index to mathematically calculate the synchronization of voice dialogue to the animated image, the director would then write these timing instructions on a series of columned charts called exposure sheets. These sheets served as a graphic guide for the animator, and also contained information pertaining to the cartoon's dialogue as well as notes on camera movements and the scene's action. By referring to the exposure sheets, the animator would draw the action to conform to the timing direction indicated on them.

For the Tom and Jerry cartoons, sound effects and music in particular were even more critical to the picture's comedic appeal than dialogue. There were occasions when Joe and I would devise a storyline in one of our cartoons that was especially designed to showcase the music. Music had certainly been the "key" element in a cartoon of which I am particularly proud called *Cat Concerto*. In this picture we decided to try and give our cat, Tom, a touch of class by casting him as a master pianist immaculately clad in white tie and tails and performing in a solo concert.

The fly in the ointment, or rather the mouse in the piano, naturally turns out to be Jerry, who mischievously disrupts the concert when his nap is disturbed by Tom's performance.

A primary factor in scoring this seven-minute picture was the selection of the piece of music that would provide the cartoon with its dominant theme. Joe and I probably spent close to two weeks listening to a number of classical piano compositions hoping to land on one that registered the right sound and feel for animation.

After a fortnight we were up to our ears in musical culture, having gone through selections by Mozart, Chopin, Beethoven, and Tchaikovsky. It was all grandly impressive, but none of it seemed to work for *Cat Concerto*. Finally, in exasperation we turned the problem over to our musical director, Scott Bradley, who in short order provided us with the perfect musical piece, Franz Liszt's *Second Hungarian Rhapsody*.

When Joe and I played the recording, we knew that it was right on the money. The various runs, staccato notes, crescendo passages, and other musical elements contained in the Liszt piece seemed from the first few bars to evoke suggestions of a rich series of possible gags for our cartoon.

Most of the action in *Cat Concerto* either took place at or within Tom's grand piano, as Tom frantically tried to nab the disruptive Jerry while at the same time attempting to continue a virtuoso performance. The hilarity of the picture depended on having the visual gags—including the little pursuits, dodges, runs, and smashes that occurred between the two characters—all orchestrated to the continuous music of the concert piece.

Once in a while you find yourself working on a certain picture when a gut feeling will surge up. Your hands will sweat and your heart will race and you know that you've somehow kicked into another gear and something special is happening creatively. That is the way I felt about the little cat-and-mouse conflict we orchestrated in *Cat Concerto*. The damned thing just seemed to take on a special life of its own and generated an oddly spontaneous symphony of musical mirth.

Nearly five decades after producing that cartoon I can view the picture and still feel the intuitive satisfaction of how that thing was timed, directed, and animated. Admittedly, that is an intensely personal reaction, but maybe the gut wasn't too far wrong since *Cat Concerto* netted us our fourth Oscar for best animated cartoon in 1947.

Along with the distinct pride I felt over the rising status of cartoonmaking as an art form, was a growing conviction within me that Joe Barbera and I were entering our majority, so to speak, as creative producers. From early on, Joe has always displayed a singular and justifiable self-confidence in his work. I have always tended to be the more introverted of our unit, but despite this reticence, I never felt that I didn't have the goods to deliver. We had both been comers when we met, and I think we knew that about each other.

By 1955, Joe and I had been partners for fifteen years, and the gratifying success of the Tom and Jerry cartoons had given us both a greater sense of personal security and confidence over our professional abilities.

Over half of my twenty-five years in professional animation up to that time had been spent at MGM, and I was relatively content in assuming that I would spend the rest of my career there as well. The little bungalow on Lot 2 where we had initially conjured with freshmen excitement back in 1940 had since evolved into a full-grown cartoon studio housed in a grand, modern two-story building that employed over a hundred people.

Admittedly, there had been numerous staff changes over the years, but that was the nature of the cartoon business. Most of the "old guard" had departed. Friz Freleng had returned to Warner Bros. Hugh Harman and Rudy Ising had for the most part retired as producers but had gone on to other studios as free-lance directors.

Most of these changes were things that you took philosophically over the years. After all, there was as much professional competition in making cartoons as there was in any other business, and we all had our own individual stars to follow. Still, it was nice to work with some of the veteran colleagues that Joe and I had started out with whenever possible. Happily, Tex Avery had remained at MGM as a producer and Michael Lah, who had worked with us on features like *Invitation to the Dance*, had also remained on board.

Although I believe that our volume of cartoon production was as prolific as any that was being turned out by other studios at the time, the variety of cartoon celebrities at MGM was not as large as at such neighboring studios as Warner Bros. Warners had developed a virtual galaxy of inkwell stars who lined up with Bugs and Daffy, including Porky Pig, Elmer Fudd, Wile E. Coyote, the Road Runner, and Bob Clampett's crowd-pleasing canary Tweety Bird.

Over at MGM, Tom and Jerry were the headliners, but during the 1950s we also featured some sparkling characters like Tex Avery's endearing hound, Droopy, and a sexy little gal Tex conjured up called Red Riding Hood for *Red Hot Riding Hood*. Droopy was to go on to enjoy a durable career as a celebrity in his own right. Unfortunately, our boss Fred Quimby considered Red Riding Hood to be a little too torrid for audiences at the time and she went into early retirement.

We might have been outnumbered, but we weren't outclassed. MGM was giving every other cartoon studio in town a run for its money in what then seemed to be at the time an accelerating bid for dominant favor with theatre audiences. That run, however, as exhilarating as it was for both Joe and me, was about to come to an end.

In 1955, Fred Quimby announced his retirement as head of the animation studio. Joe and I were first saddened by the news and then astonished when we learned that Fred had appointed us as his successors. Hal Elias would continue on as the business supervisor, but Joe and I were designated to head the creative end of production.

I was deeply moved by Fred's decision and display of confidence in our abilities. Joe and I had been the beardless rookies among the cadre of cartoonmakers who had first answered Quimby's call back in 1940. We had been there since the studio's inception, and I imagine that this longevity along with the success of our creations pretty much explained the reasoning behind this passing of the torch.

Beyond this professional protocol, however, things proceeded pretty much the way they always had. Joe and I assumed the reins, but we held them lightly. It turned out to be a fairly simple job of management. Tex and Mike both were gifted and competent producers. Although Joe and I looked at everything they did, we were generally very comfortable in letting them exercise their creative judgment and we both felt that everything they turned out was fine.

These halcyon days were pleasant, but alas, fated to be numbered. Although most of us involved in animation production did not know it at the time, the theatrical cartoon as a commercial product had entered an irreversible decline. By the 1950s television had made impressive inroads in the entertainment industry and was captivating an increasingly larger audience. As motion picture production costs rose and profits eroded, studios—including MGM—

somberly assessed their liabilities and implacably decided to discontinue all cartoon production. The business reasoning, we learned later, was that the executives felt that the studio had acquired enough cartoons in their library to enable them to recirculate them in sales to theatres, and decided to curtail further costs by halting the production of any additional cartoons.

One morning early in 1957, the phone rang and the ax fell. We were told that MGM had decided to close its cartoon studio. We were instructed to finish up production of whatever cartoons we were making as quickly as possible and to lay everyone off. The announcement came completely out of the blue. There was a stunned silence from everyone, and then a kind of general choked exhalation of disbelief. "Oh my God!"

It was heartbreaking to face a hundred and ten people who you worked with so closely and suddenly tell them that they were all fired. What could we say that was really worth saying beyond the inescapable lousy news? Apologies are a hollow thing, and in that first seizure of despair the mind has a tough time trying to grasp any notion that might offer the merest glimmer of hope. The pronouncement was absolute. They won't reconsider, we are all finished here, it is over.

Besides, Joe and I were in the same boat and it was sinking. To be metaphorically more precise, we were sitting at the top with no mountain under us. In a time of crisis, it is the most human thing in the world to search for a scapegoat and curse the thing as a way of draining your wound. The culprit in this case seemed to be an innocuous-looking little electrical box called television.

Neither Joe nor I cursed—not for long anyway. Instead, we considered. Television could either be our doom or our possible deliverance. While we cleaned out our desks we also pondered. We were damned good at what we did. If we couldn't make cartoons for the big screen anymore, then why not try and sell them to the small screen? By the time our office was vacant and we had to "turn in the keys," Joe Barbera and I had come to one major decision.

We might have to give up MGM, relinquish our creation of Tom and Jerry to the studio and renounce our positions as heads of production, but there was one thing we would not have to give up if we chose, and that was our partnership. It had worked for nearly eighteen years and somehow, some way, we'd continue to make it work.

We weren't through yet.

The famous frontiersman Davy Crockett was known to have a favorite motto: "Be sure you're right, then go ahead." As Joe and I pondered the uncertain prospects of television animation production, we both concluded that neither of us could afford Davy's precautionary luxury. Right or wrong, there was only one direction we could go and that was ahead. We decided to take that course together.

Chapter Seven

All the Right Moves

Old habits are hard to break. After eighteen years of getting up at six a.m. every morning and making the thirty-minute drive to work at Culver City, it was disconcerting and a little baffling to confront daily the need to retool a professional lifestyle and take a detour route to one's future. As we wound up the final production work during our last weeks at MGM, Joe and I discussed our options for new work quarters. We needed a base and a location from which we could develop a product and generate a market.

Admittedly, it was a little like putting the cart before the horse. We were scouting for a place of business without having a business to go into. Yet this was not quite as impractical as it seemed. Joe and I were working on a notion and if it worked, as we were convinced it would, we would soon be busier than hell.

A few weeks after the MGM cartoon unit closed, we re-situated ourselves in offices at Charlie Chaplin's studio located at La Brea and Sunset Boulevard. It was an old lot formerly owned by the legendary Little Tramp himself, but a new and exciting environment for two guys about to hang up their own shingle. Well, we had the nail and hammer ready…but what were we going to put on that shingle?

There was a brief discussion and no debate. Because I was short of cash, Joe pulled out a half dollar from his pocket and flipped the coin. Heads, Barbera and Hanna, or tails, Hanna-Barbera. The coin spun and landed, clattering on the linoleum floor. It was tails.

Thus christened, our partnership formed the core around which Joe and I planned to build a fledgling animation company geared exclusively to the production of cartoons for television. There were no forerunners in this field, no established precedents of production methods or marketing—and no assurances of success. Although *Crusader Rabbit* was created for television way back in 1949, it was a unique production among recycled theatrical cartoons. And certainly no company was risking all to simply create TV animation. Television, for anyone aspiring to produce custom-made cartoons for the medium, was still a no man's land, but it was also an open field and that suited Joe and me just fine.

Neither of us were daunted by the logistics of such an operation. Both Joe and I felt that we knew how to build a successful cartoon studio. After all, we had just walked away from a nearly twenty-year endeavor that accomplished that very thing at Metro-Goldwyn-Mayer. There were two major differences this time, however.

One: This enterprise was to be the formation of our *own* studio. Two: It was *our* money that was riding on the venture.

As it was, it wasn't a vast fortune of money either, but it was all we had. Eighteen years of steady employment had paid for the house that Vi and I had built back in 1940, and slowly nourished a modest but respectable savings account. Vi and I discussed the imminent transition in our lives and took stock of our assets. We would in effect be mortgaging our future on helping to underwrite the new cartoon company of Hanna-Barbera and Violet knew it.

"What we'd have to do is to spend the money we've taken half our lives to save," I told her. Vi was undismayed. She picked up the slender bank book and pushed it across the coffee table to me. "Well then, Bill," she said, "we'll spend it on the second half."

In order to subsidize Hanna-Barbera, Joe and I pooled our resources and managed to come up with about $30,000. This left both of us with lunch money for about a month, if we ate lightly. The money was invested primarily in leasing our offices at the studio, acquiring the basic inking and painting and film editing and sound facilities, and hiring a core staff of artists and animators who were gleaned mostly from our original staff at MGM.

Joe had been working on storyboards for a possible new team of cartoon characters we had discussed, and I thought the sketches showed exciting promise. Having bid fond adieu to our erstwhile cat-and-mouse team, we decided to change cartoon "tails" a bit and came up with a new duo composed of a cat named "Ruff" and a dog named

"Reddy." The names of these characters speak volumes about the dispositions of their two creators, for Joe and I were working with exhaustive intensity on devising a new production process calculated to make Ruff and Reddy the demonstration models for a whole new method of cartoon animation.

All of this innovative ardor, I will confess, funneled down to a basic case of necessity being the mother of invention. The high cost of production had sounded the death knell for theatrical cartoons at MGM, and the bell had begun to toll at Warner and Disney as well. Producing animation for television was not only our brightest prospect, it was our *only* alternative.

In order to crack the market, we needed to cut expenses drastically. Projected production budgets were niggardly enough for regular live-action television programs, but they were downright meagre for prospective TV cartoons. Shortly before the studio closed at MGM, Joe and I had submitted one earnest bid to MGM executives attempting to convince them to retain their cartoon unit for television production. After a quick review and evaluation of the average production costs incurred in turning out the full-animation pictures we'd done with Tom and Jerry, I composed a six-page memo explaining how such costs could be cut by at least half by employing a system of limited animation that used fewer drawings and required less inking and painting, less camera work—in fact, less of everything except background art.

In today's phraseology, that would be called "crunching the numbers." They were pretty persuasive figures, I'll have to admit. I had the damned thing typed up and sent the memo off to Hal Elias with a flourish. I don't believe that we ever heard a word from him.

In the midst of this silent rejection, one cheerful note sounded. Over the years working at MGM, Joe and I had developed a friendship with George Sidney, who we first came to know while working together on *Anchors Aweigh*. George had since come to be regarded as one of the studio's most talented motion picture directors. On the flip side of the coin, Joe and I had managed to develop a fair reputation of our own as a couple of creative guys with a respectable track record for producing the award-winning cartoon series for MGM. Sidney had on occasion listened to Joe and me discuss our limited animation concept and enthusiastically affirmed a belief in its possibilities for television production.

A little validation is nice, but we needed a deal. Sidney pondered a bit and came up with a proposition. George was impressively connected among various agencies in town and suggested that now was the time to shop the circuit. He would act as a business representative for us. In return for setting up a meeting with a prospective financial backer for our new cartoon product and a small financial investment in Hanna-Barbera Productions, Sidney would take a small percentage of our company. Joe and I considered. It was a chance at least, maybe a pretty damned good one. We agreed to the deal.

Sidney proved to be as good as his word. A few days later we got a call from George advising us that he had scheduled a meeting with programming executives at Screen Gems. Joe and I were primed for the pitch. We both knew that Screen Gems had been considering entering the television animation market. When we learned that their executives were less than enchanted by the development of an earlier cartoon series proposed by a couple of other animators, our hopes soared.

We knew we had come up with a winning cartoon package that could make converts out of skeptics. What's more, I had in my pocket a streamlined production budget for making those cartoons that I was convinced would virtually sell itself.

By the time we'd set up our new offices, I had honed down the projected costs of making a six-minute television cartoon from the original $17,500 estimated earlier in my aborted proposal to the MGM management to approximately $3000. During the years that Joe and I had produced Tom and Jerry, we had been given a budget of about $35,000 for each seven-minute fully animated cartoon we turned out.

By utilizing our new method of limited animation, we were convinced that *Ruff and Reddy* could be aired as a cartoon series on television for about one-tenth of that cost. How could they resist? We were fairly confident that they could not.

As it turned out, Screen Gems did not resist, although Joe and I had to do a little relenting as far as the money was concerned. We could tell almost immediately that they liked our storyboards and the show's concept. The characters were appealing, and an original animated series would provide TV some badly needed refreshment from the stale programming recourse of constantly rerunning old theatrical cartoons.

Still, as it was repeatedly explained to us, the money that could be allocated for such experimental broadcasts was extremely tight. Television executives seemed to feel, probably quite justifiably, that it was incumbent upon them to squeeze every dollar until the eagle screamed.

By the time that Joe and I walked out of that office, however, we had our deal. As it turned out, it cost us about twenty percent of our company, but in return for this concession, Screen Gems gave us an option to produce five five-minute cartoons. The first two for $2700 apiece, the second two for $2800, and the fifth for $3000.

Ruff and Reddy was slated to be the opening and closing acts for a half-hour children's show that aired on Saturday afternoons. The show was hosted by a live host co-starring with puppets, and also featured reruns of old Columbia theatrical cartoons.

Joe and I had pooled our thirty grand to subsidize Hanna-Barbera Productions. We now had to combine every bit of our respective professional abilities and experience in cartoonmaking to devise the costwise and creatively innovative system of limited animation. Since we were financially limited to the number of drawings that could be produced in animating *Ruff and Reddy*, it was essential that we select only the key poses necessary to convincingly impart the illusion of movement in our cartoons.

It would be flattering to claim that the development of our limited animation process was akin to re-inventing the wheel in cartoonmaking. I think it a more apt description to say, however, that we installed a new gear in the system. All of the elements that would ultimately be incorporated in television cartoons had been present in theatrical cartoons. There was movement, sound, dialogue, and music. Another key factor to be considered as critical to our cartoon production was the use of color. Despite the fact that TV shows were then being broadcast in black and white, Joe and I could see color programming looming on the television horizon. That dawn would bring a rainbow and Joe and I resolved to be prepared when it came, by deciding to go ahead and produce the Ruff and Reddy cartoons in color.

All of the essential components would be there. They would just be allotted in a different proportion for television. Fundamentally, we still needed to turn out a cartoon product that would be funny and fun to watch. The characters had to have personality and project the kind of appeal that would grow on an audience. They needed to have the right look in form and color and to be presented to viewers in environmental backgrounds imaginative and colorful enough to especially captivate children. The storylines needed to be as interesting as those in theatrical cartoons and the gags just as clever. Most inescapably, however, it all had to be done initially by Joe and me for $2700 a cartoon.

In general, the process of producing a cartoon using limited animation was essentially the same as producing a fully animated cartoon. A script for the cartoon was written and a storyboard was drawn depicting in a series of key illustrations or scenes the basic action of the cartoon's story. After the material had been developed on the storyboards, the dialogue was then recorded, providing a soundtrack for the cartoon.

The storyboards were then photographed frame by frame and processed on film along with the soundtrack to create the pose reel that Joe and I had used to such good advantage by previewing these scenes in sequence to develop the proposed action for our Tom and Jerry cartoons. It had proved particularly valuable to me as a kind of test film that gave me a sense of the timing necessary to pace the action frame by frame for animating the cartoon.

A stringent budget of $2700 per cartoon, however, would only buy us a fraction of the artwork that we had used for our theatrical productions. Back at MGM our budget was lavish enough to allow as many as sixty drawings per foot of fully animated film. It was a new ballgame for TV. In order to meet our budget for *Ruff and Reddy*, we had to pare the drawings down to no more than one or two per foot of film.

In viewing the selected drawings on our pose reel, Joe and I realized that the sequence of these pencil drawings could effectively suggest the humor and action of the cartoon even before it was animated. We reasoned that by animating only key poses and selected drawings that dramatized or emphasized the cartoon's dialogue, we could artfully reduce the overall amount of drawings used in a television cartoon and still produce the convincing illusion of movement in the film.

This was a process that we felt was eminently right for the television medium. The creative nature of television programming during those early days quite naturally stressed intimacy rather than spectacle. The perspective of an audience sitting in their living rooms watching a TV program on a (standard-dimension) screen was entirely different from that of an audience sitting before a vast wide-angled screen in a theatre.

Joe and I had gained a foretaste of that back at MGM, when we had screened pose reels in a projection room with some of the kids we worked with. Very often we had all found these pictures to be as funny as the finished cartoon itself. In many respects the selective animation we planned to produce for TV emulated many of the live-action films that were shown both in theatres and television. Economizing on our artwork, we elected to rely heavily on close-ups, alternating occasionally to a full shot or medium shot to give pace to the sequences. The key drawings for these shots were designed to depict the character in poses expressive enough to emphasize their dialogue.

By streamlining the process in this manner, we could use key scenes to evoke the planned action necessary to make our cartoons move aided by the use of an efficiently reduced number of intermediate drawings. In addition, we would have to introduce well-written scripts to provide our characters with the clever and funny dialogue necessary to bring them convincingly to life.

Following these principles, Joe and I simply proceeded in production to define and refine the process by doing what seemed to come naturally. For *Ruff and Reddy* we eliminated detailed backgrounds that we knew would not effectively project on the TV screen, and developed simpler yet colorful and visually appealing settings for our characters.

In streamlining these production methods, both Joe and I felt impelled virtually from the day we got our deal at Screen Gems to direct these tactics toward turning out a quality cartoon. We may have had to cut costs, pinch pennies, and re-tool the animation system, but it was all geared toward putting a program on the market that we felt would ultimately be worth the television viewer's time to watch.

After all, Joe Barbera and I had earned a solid reputation as good cartoonmakers, and we wanted to protect that professional respect. *Ruff and Reddy* was to be the premier product for the company of Hanna-Barbera and there was no percentage in turning out crap just to prove we could meet a budget. The challenge was to use the means at hand and, with the application of whatever ingenuity we could conjure, conceive something that was new, exciting, and had enough creative potential to grow with television itself. The integrity of a cartoon's audience is that virtually anyone from the age of six or seven years on up will be able to tell from viewing six minutes of film if your picture was funny and magical enough to be worth watching.

Ruff and Reddy developed into a team of very likable characters that I thought would appeal to kids in both their looks and personalities. Most of the major animation characters appearing in theatres had traditionally been for the most part solo acts starring in their own cartoons with "guest star appearances" by other personalities. Disney had employed this format with most of its characters, including Mickey, Donald, Goofy, and most of the others. Warner had done the same with Bugs and company.

There were exceptions, of course, with such rival duos as the Road Runner and Wile E. Coyote and Sylvester and Tweety. Joe and I had always liked this kind of ongoing comedic rapport between characters, and variations of the "buddy theme" were to become a consistent element in our cartoons throughout our career.

Tom and Jerry, of course, had been friendly rivals. In Ruff and Reddy we decided to eliminate the nemesis factor and make the two characters best friends. Consequently, this softer relationship placed a greater emphasis on the humor and wit conveyed to the audience through dialogue between the two characters.

While working on the storyboards, I decided to indulge my fondness for writing verse and try to come up with some catchy lyrics for the theme song for our new show. The idea was to compose some little ditty that would catch the viewer's ear and capture the spirit of our characters in a few fun phrases.

One morning I scrounged up some sheet music and a pencil and started scribbling. A couple of cups of strong black coffee with extra sugar seemed to fuel my muse, and about an hour later I handed the lyrics to our musical director, Hoyt Curtin, who obligingly composed a bright little melody in accompaniment. The results of my early morning exercise ran as follows:

> Get set Get ready
> Here comes Ruff and Reddy
> They're tough but steady
> Always Ruff and Reddy
>
> They sometimes have their little spats
> Even fight like dogs and cats
> But when they need each other
> That's when they're Ruff and Reddy

That was my first fling as a lyricist. Although I didn't give it much thought at the time, it was to pretty much set the pattern for my writing the theme song lyrics for Hanna-Barbera cartoon shows for the next thirty years.

Because Ruff and Reddy were to be the first major personalities created by Hanna-Barbera to speak, casting the perfect voices for these guys became a main priority. We had worked with numerous voice artists back at MGM and knew we could call in a lot of talent to audition. After listening to numerous recordings, we finally cast two exceptional talents, Don Messick and Daws Butler. Joe and I felt their voice characterizations captured respectively the personalities of cocky little Ruff and the good-natured, unflappable Reddy to a tee.

While still in preproduction, Joe and I learned that our new series was to be aired as a part of the NBC Network's Saturday afternoon line-up. A few weeks later, we were introduced to John Mitchell, at the time head of sales for Columbia Pictures, the parent company of Screen Gems. John was a dynamic salesman, energetic, personable, and an ardent believer in the commercial potential of our limited animation product. Mitchell was one of the earliest converts to this cause among studio executives in the industry. This zeal, combined with his gifted drive as a salesman, was to significantly advance the promotion of Hanna-Barbera Productions in those early years.

Ruff and Reddy premiered on NBC December 14, 1957 with a debut episode titled *Planet Pirates*. Although we had screened the picture before broadcast, I have to admit that I was somewhat concerned over how the final product would actually work when aired. To my great relief, however, all of our theories worked well, and I saw that limited animation actually came off better on the dimly lit television screen than the old fully animated things.

Inner relief turned into open elation the next morning when Joe and I read reviews in the trade papers, which gave high marks to *Ruff and Reddy* as an entertaining and clever cartoon program. The most thrilling validation of our efforts, however, came when NBC signed us to a five-year contract to produce and develop additional cartoon series for television. The picture was brightening, we were convinced, not only for Hanna-Barbera Productions but for the future of television itself.

Joe and I had inaugurated our careers in television cartoon production with the basic premise that "less means more." Because of the fewer drawings we used, the new process was dubbed "limited animation" by critics. In my mind, however, that phrase has always been somewhat of a paradox in terms. Limited may have meant fewer drawings per foot of film, but the concept that Joe and I launched was hardly restrictive in either its creative or commercial potential. As far as Joe and I were concerned, limited animation was the wave of the future. It offered an expansive format that challenged us to make all the right moves in the selection of key images, timing, and the development of clever dialogue and creative voice characterizations.

It was all a matter of perspective. For many of us who knew and loved cartoons, the term "limited animation" hardly conveyed the expansive spirit of its initiative and vision any more than the reference to television as the "small screen" augured the huge potential growth of an exciting new communication medium. For the team of Hanna-Barbera, however, those two phrases opened up a whole new field of innovative production that gave us room to grow.

Avice Denby Hanna with me *(seated right)* and my sisters Lucille, Constance, and Norma. Around 1913.

A proud Boy Scout in 1924.

I'm holding my sister Marion with Norma around 1914.

1927

Ready for the future—in my plus fours. Los Angeles, 1928.

The newlyweds, August 7, 1936.

With my father, William John Hanna, in 1943.

Our family in 1943: Bonnie, Violet, David, and me.

David took to scouting much like the Old Man. 1948.

Bonnie in 1949.

The cartoon studio at MGM. *(C. G. Maxwell)*

Joe Barbera

Joe's first sketches of Jasper and Jinx for *Puss Gets the Boot* (1939).

Tom and Jerry—our animated partners at MGM for seventeen years.
(© *Turner Entertainment Co.*)

Tom and Jerry in the Academy-Award-winning *Cat Concerto*. (© *Turner Entertainment Co.*)

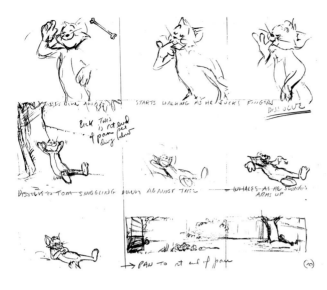

A Joe Barbera storyboard for Tom and Jerry.

Hugh Harman (left) and cameraman Jack Stevens at MGM.

Rudy Ising looks over the work of animator W.D. Burness.

Working with Dick Bickenbach in 1946.

Joe and I entertain a studio visitor—child star Margaret O'Brien—in 1946.

MGM cartoon chief Fred Quimby *(near right)* isn't sure what to make of our antics as we show him the story for *Mouse in Manhattan*.

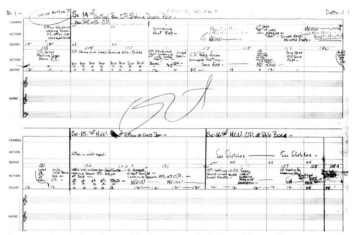

An example of a bar sheet with the cartoon's timing, this one from *Officer Pooch*.

A model sheet for Tom by Irv Spence.

Tex Avery was an animation legend I was proud to work with at MGM— and later at Hanna-Barbera in 1979. Here at MGM with Fred Quimby looking over his shoulder.

The Tom and Jerry team with their Oscars in 1952 (*left to right*): Ed Barge, Irv Spence, Dick Bickenbach, Joe Barbera, me, and Ken Muse.

Esther Williams finds two animated swimming companions in *Dangerous When Wet* (1953). (© *Turner Entertainment Co.*)

Anchors Aweigh
(© *Turner Entertainment Co.*)

Gene Kelly and Jerry Mouse create a little magic in *Anchors Aweigh*. (© *Turner Entertainment Co.*)

Invitation to the Dance—Gene Kelly's ambitious dance/animation sequence. (© *Turner Entertainment Co.*)

Invitation to the Dance.
(© *Turner Entertainment Co.*)

Chapter Eight

A One Dog Night

lthough I must confess to being no great reader of novels, I do recall once coming across a couple of lines in a book that pretty much described how things went for Hanna-Barbera Productions following the sale of *Ruff and Reddy*. The one phrase that stands out from an otherwise vague reading experience went something like, "From that moment, events rapidly unfolded." And that was pretty much the way it was. Selling our first show to television was like the first olive out of the bottle.

With a five-year contract to develop cartoon shows for a major network and a gung-ho business representative like John Mitchell eager to push their sale, Joe and I launched into the intense process of conceiving and developing a succession of original and new cartoon properties for TV at a pace that made the production schedule we'd maintained back at MGM appear leisurely.

Joe, being the artistic half of our team, had his creative steam up and was turning out sketches for new characters at a rate of what seemed about one every five minutes. How he did it I'll never know. Joe was magic with a pencil in his hand.

Looking back now, I can recall those early bull sessions with him in our office as being some of the most enjoyable times of our career. Just as we had during those years at MGM, my partner and I sat together with a desk between us and discussed with a heated zeal the concepts for new characters and shows.

Despite our outward display of self-assurance and a legitimate reserve of inner confidence, Joe and I both knew that we were basically infants as independent producers in the TV business. We had our contract and we had our offices, but in many respects we were basically winging it, inventing ourselves and our company as we went along.

Included in that fledgling Hanna-Barbera company were approximately 150 people who had worked with us at MGM. Less than three months after the gates of that studio had slammed on all of us, Joe and I had assembled these folks into our own production ranks, assigned them to work on the first Ruff and Reddy cartoons, and paid them salaries out of the grubstake money from our own pockets.

The creative concepts for our shows could be worked out by Joe and me and a core unit of layout people at our offices, but the lot itself was too small to house our entire staff. In order to provide adequate facilities for our inkers and painters, we leased two additional buildings on La Brea Avenue in Hollywood to be used as studios.

The other major production aspects, such as the camera work, recording, and editing functions, would be handled by engaging subcontractors. Needless to say, Joe and I were anxious to centralize all of our departments in a single studio as soon as we could. For the present, however, it was heartening just to have our old colleagues reunited and working with us.

During our years at MGM neither Joe nor I had ever been faced with the necessity of selling our own shows in order to stay in business. Now we had to create a market for ourselves and hustle our—well, hustle, really scramble to expand that market.

Guys like John Mitchell had helped open our eyes to that. John was a hot spur. He dug the rowels into us, relentlessly urging, coaxing, cajoling, and demanding that we seize the day, day after day, in varying and expanding our production menu for the ravenous programming needs of TV.

Mitchell would suddenly appear in our office immaculately clad in a Brooks Brothers suit, always looking as if he'd just been to the barbershop. Joe and I were burning a lot of midnight oil in those days and often scarcely bothered to shave. The two of us would look up, disheveled and bleary-eyed from our boards, sketches, or notes, and listen with respectful weariness while the debonair and driven Mitchell exhorted us on. "What you guys have to come up with is an arsenal of new and different cartoon shows, each of them with winning characters. Stars! Stars like Tom and Jerry! Stars like Ruff & Reddy. Make them any way you'd like, but by God make 'em stars!"

A moment later he'd be en route somewhere, presumably to some agency featuring plush front offices and a suite, in order to pitch a potential deal for two grizzled guys in shirt-sleeves who called themselves Hanna-Barbera.

As Joe and I grappled with the demands of gaining "industrial strength" as a company, our respective duties and roles as partners became defined with vivid clarity. After working together for nearly twenty years, we knew our respective creative assets. I undertook the production end of the business, which involved timing the scenes and working with the artists and animators to turn out the cartoons. Joe developed into the salesman of our unit, an undertaking that complemented his natural powers of persuasion to perfection. He developed a phenomenal flair for marketing our shows that netted us a bounty of network sales almost from the onset.

Events had indeed rapidly unfolded in this latest chapter of our careers and as we plunged ahead, the plot thickened. Six months earlier the demise of theatrical cartoons had left Joe and me holding a bag full of lemons. Now, figuratively speaking, we had one of the first lemonade stands on the block, selling our product to a television clientele with an apparently unquenchable thirst.

Who could ask for anything better? Well, if the whole truth were to be told, Joe and I could. Cracking the TV market with a customized, cost-effective cartoon was great, but if Hanna-Barbera was to stay on the market, we needed to cultivate a thriving business relationship with that ever vital provider of financial backing called the sponsor.

In order to do this, we had to sweeten our sales prospects by coming up with a different program format. *Ruff and Reddy* had been sold as a "wrap-around" deal that provided the bread for a show that sandwiched in between a mixture of other variety entertainment.

Well, if we could sell two cartoons for a half-hour show, why couldn't we sell *three* and increase our sales by over thirty percent for a single package deal? With a draftsman like Joe Barbera, it was never a case of having to go back to the drawing board for new characters and concepts. Joe never left the drawing board, or to put it more precisely, he never really required one. A pencil and sketchpad was all he needed to graphically develop our concepts; within three weeks, we had storyboards for the introduction of a trio of new cartoon shows headlined by a likable, sleepy-eyed blue canine named Huckleberry Hound.

The challenge before us now was to unleash our amiable hound on the critical hunt for a sponsor. With *Ruff and Reddy* as our bread-and-butter show, we apportioned what revenue we could from that series to finance the production of a pilot cartoon of Huck and dug into our savings for the rest. Turning out our first series had taught Joe and me some invaluable lessons regarding meeting production schedules and how best to efficiently allocate time to produce each element of the cartoon.

We used these techniques to good advantage in refining the schedule involved with producing *Huckleberry Hound*, and expedited the whole creative process from concept to completion. By late spring of 1958, we had the half-hour pilot for *The Huckleberry Hound Show* in the can, with John Mitchell and Joe Barbera primed for the pitch. This was to be Joe's debut as our company's salesperson. I was both heartened by his buoyant confidence and relieved in the knowledge that *I* would not have to be the guy selling the picture.

The always dynamic and persuasive Mitchell had pulled off the impressive coup of selling the idea of the *The Huckleberry Hound Show* to the Kellogg cereal company over the telephone. But it was left to Joe to clinch the deal with a sales presentation.

As far as Joe and I were concerned, my partner was well-armed with the makings of a great variety half-hour cartoon show that he could pitch from his heart. In addition to Huck, we had come up with a squadron of new characters for two other seven-minute cartoons. The first one featured a pair of mischievous mice named Pixie and Dixie teamed opposite a perennial nemesis in the form of a cat named Mr. Jinx. The third cartoon debuted a cocky, bon-vivant bruin named Yogi Bear and his sidekick Boo Boo.

As it turned out, my partner needed every ounce of his pluck and panache in that first New York sales conference. Joe had been slated to present our package to a long gray line of executives from the Kellogg's people and their public relation representatives from the Leo Burnett Agency. The conference could hardly have had a more inauspicious start. Confronted with an assembly of impatient, business-weary people who seemed in no mood for anything other than getting on to an overdue luncheon, Joe could see that he had his work cut out for him. It was hardly a captive audience, but Joe was undismayed. He'd win them over.

The projector was set up and our star duo of mice, Pixie and Dixie, were set to be previewed. Joe pushed the button and a moment later gave an inward groan. Just as the film began to roll, he realized that the wrong soundtrack had been used. Pixie and Dixie were up there on the screen all right, but they were speaking in the voice of Yogi Bear!

Joe had visions of our prospects being shot down in flames right then and there. Who could blame him? Never one to admit defeat, he quickly switched soundtracks and began the film again. The mice, and then our bear, and finally our noble hound dog, Huck, began to work their wiles on the audience. Joe could feel their resistance soften. Twenty minutes later the room was roaring with laughter. Joe had sold the show.

The Huckleberry Hound Show premiered on KPIX in New York on October 2, 1958. Joe and I scanned the reviews, scrutinized the ratings, and at length allowed ourselves to be carried along on the first wave of elation as the show gave every indication of becoming a smash hit. The blue canine with the red bow tie, sleepy eyes, and southern drawl had made good. Huckleberry Hound was on his way to becoming television's first cartoon superstar.

A great part of Huck's star appeal to viewers, I think, came from a down-home, straight-arrow personality that made him so doggone lovable. Huck's low-key, ambling attitude was particularly suited to our limited animation methods at the time, which stressed less movement and more dialogue to impart personality to the characters. Huck's voice was sheer magic. The laid-back, sow-belly-and-greens accent that Daws Butler endowed the character complemented perfectly the visual image of our unflappable little idealist.

Huckleberry Hound, of course, had a great ensemble cast which helped put the whole show over the top. Yogi Bear, Pixie and Dixie, and Mr. Jinx were to all emerge as distinct personalities of their own, creating a special kind of cartoon chemistry that worked for the whole show.

Now and again when nostalgia moves me, I'll run some of those original episodes and still find them to be some of the funniest and most entertaining cartoons we've ever made. The quality of work is always representative of the quality of the workers, and we began, I believe, with some of the best in the business.

I was a doting pet owner, and my favorite command to our dog, Rags, was the encouragement to speak. Since Huck was our top dog in television, it was particularly critical that he not only speak, but converse constantly and cleverly. In those days we had three gifted writers, Warren Foster, Charlie Shows, and Mike Maltese, working to come up with the story and script material that provided Huck and all the others with those humorous lines and situations.

While the scribes put their words into scripts, the rest of our units hustled to do what they were best at. Veteran animators like Irv Spence and Ray Patterson quickly adjusted to the limited animation concept and proceeded to develop the principles into an art form of its own with remarkable ingenuity.

This creative adaptability applied to everyone involved in production. When guys like Daws Butler and Don Messick launched into their uncanny voice characterizations for Yogi, Mr. Jinx, and the others, we knew that our whole cast along with Huck were on their way to becoming small-screen celebrities.

It was exciting stuff for all of us, particularly for two guys named Bill and Joe who were just beginning to get used to the notion that after making the payroll, they might start writing themselves a salary check or two.

And then one evening in 1959, something happened that encouraged Joe Barbera and me to think we could probably cash those checks with less personal anxiety. On that night the two of us donned the unaccustomed formal apparel of tuxedos and accepted the Television Academy Award as the producers of the first animated cartoon series to receive an Emmy Award.

Eight years had passed since that afternoon when Joe and I and some colleagues had posed in Fred Quimby's office for a photograph with the Oscars we'd watched Fred collect for seven Academy Award ceremonies. The winner then had been the cat-and-mouse team that Joe and I had created for movies. Now it was television, and this was our turn to take the podium. Only this time the cartoon star being honored at the gala was a modest, "shucks folks" hound. Call it karma, call it luck, or just call it pluck. With our hound Huck we learned that sooner or later, every dog will have his day—or night.

Chapter Nine

Developing Character

One of the vital elements necessary to rouse an audience's enthusiasm for a TV cartoon show is fanfare. This generally means opening the show with a musical composition known as the "main title" or the show's theme song. My own enthusiasm for the growing popularity of *The Huckleberry Hound Show* was probably most blatantly expressed in the wide-open lyrics I composed for the show's musical entry.

> The big-gest show in town
> Is Huck-le-berry Hound
> For all you guys and gals
>
> The big-gest clown in town
> Is Huck-le-berry Hound
> With all his car-toon pals

All very well. We may have believed Huckleberry to be the biggest show in town, but in order to insure that we would continue to make the payroll, Hanna-Barbera would have to hustle up new cartoon concepts to make sure that it did not remain the *only* show in town.

The television business in certain respects is like a crapshoot. Hit series, no matter how bright their prospects may appear, are never guaranteed to remain so indefinitely. Huck looked like a solid success, but so had our eighteen-year career at MGM with Tom and Jerry. We had our foot in the door with television now, and when the foot's in the door, you *push*.

It also helps to have a little leverage when you have at it, and this is when it became apparent that my partner's exceptional gift for developing story concepts could provide us with that vital momentum. Joe and I had never been concerned with the formal allocation of duties or functions in our partnership. We had always mutually and respectively done what came naturally. This creative informality had not only helped us to become more self-defined as individuals over the years, but had enhanced the growth of our business association as well.

What came naturally to both Joe and me was improvising, and what evolved during those first months following the sale of Huck was an offhand division of labor that appeared to work well despite its lack of any formal design. While I concentrated on the logistics of production, Joe, in addition to handling the sale of our shows, also assumed the function of working with our writers in developing the concepts for new cartoon shows.

By this time we had gathered an impressive corps of talent, and Joe developed the remarkable knack of playing this diversity like a violin. It was probably inevitable that many of the Hanna-Barbera cartoon characters that emerged at the time often directly reflected a lot of the quirks and personality traits of the writers themselves.

Joe had a bead on the artistic forte of each guy on the team, and used this insight to put the best writer on the show best suited to his talent. The result was a creative alignment that I think imparted a freshness and originality not only to the shows themselves, but to each character we developed as well. It was good management, and it brought out creative dimensions in our writing staff that were free-wheeling, spontaneous, and often absurdly creative.

Joe and I still reminisce about those formative days when so many of our most popular characters and shows were conceived. In a recent discussion, my partner reminded me of the creative diversity of many of our original writers and old friends that brought back vivid memories of them as unique individuals.

"I remember it like this, Bill. I had to cast the cartoon show for the best writer. It was like casting actors for a movie. We would select the writers who had the best technique for a particular show.

"My take on Mike Maltese was that he had a very smart-aleck approach to his humor. He had a way with words, especially clever rhyme phrases like 'Quick Draw McGraw,' or employing catchy phrases like Snagglepuss's 'Exit, stage left!' All that stuff worked for our jauntier characters. At other times I'd go with Warren Foster, who had a better sense of story, or Tony Benedict, who was a great gag man."

Once the concepts were introduced, Joe would go over the stories with the writer, rework the storyboard, and eventually direct the actors when they recorded the dialogue. What evolved from this process were many of the nuances, quirks, gags, trademarks, and voice accents that gave debut characters like Quick Draw McGraw, Baba Looey, Loopey de Loop, Augie Doggie and Doggie Daddy, and others the standout personalities we hoped would make them hits with the television audience.

One of the questions people have asked me the most often regarding our shows is this: What are the qualities that make a winning television cartoon personality? That is both an easy and at the same time very difficult thing to answer. In general, I've always felt that any character we presented to the audience had to project a presence of some kind that would somehow interest or excite the viewer.

The ability to evoke "audience response" is a primary index for gauging the prospective success of any cartoon show, and every member of the cast must be an effective contributor. Evaluating the star appeal of a cartoon character is as difficult to describe in precise terms as it is to explain the charisma of a live-action actor. It is a quality composed of both an intangible essence and specific mechanics.

The artistic design of our cartoon characters was guided by a number of definite factors that experience had taught us worked visually. From a general standpoint, we wanted our characters to have a pleasing and congenial appearance that would appeal to children.

What this meant to Joe and me was that any dog, cat, wolf, bird, or any other creature conceived for a show should by its look arouse interest or excitement in a child, but never fear or revulsion. Cuteness, of course, was always a staple. Personally, I always thought that Huck, Pixie and Dixie, Yogi Bear, and many of the others that followed them always rated high on the "cuddling" scale. They had a cozy, lovable look that kids could take to their hearts.

Not every cartoon character, however, can be a "warm fuzzy" if the cast is to have creative diversity. Heroes like Huck and Quick

Draw McGraw had to contend with an assortment of nemeses, including ghosts, bandits, stern authority figures, and other adversaries if their adventures were to captivate the viewers.

In designing the look of these characters, our artists would work meticulously to create a visual presentation that complemented the tone of the show and enhanced the cast with personalities that appeared to be humorous and fun, if not always sympathetic. Conflict was, of course, a key story element in many of our cartoons, but we endeavored to depict such rivalry through harmless action rather than violence.

Cartoons have always had their abundant share of good guys and bad guys. The heavies cast in our cartoons at Hanna-Barbera, however, were more in the nature of antagonists than actual villains. Even the bad guys were never strictly evil, nor did they ever really look that sinister.

Good or bad, nasty or nice, to their creators, cartoon personalities are in many ways like their own children. We conceive them, watch them grow and develop, and celebrate with pride their success and popularity. Over the years both Joe and I have met countless viewers who have expressed avid curiosity about our own personal favorites among the legions of characters we've created. This is a fair enough question, for quite candidly, both of us have spent our entire careers wondering the same thing about our audience.

Quite predictably I think our mutual and heartfelt response is in acknowledging as our first love Tom and Jerry. My special pal among our later television cast is a blustery guy who is waiting in the wings of this book and who will appear shortly.

For Joe, however, the character nearest his heart has always been an Epicurean bear with a porkpie hat named Yogi. In many respects I think Joe and Yogi Bear are kindred spirits. They share an endearing kind of optimistic and urbane love for the good life—a love that, through my long association with Yogi, and even longer association with Joe, I've discovered appears to be for both a kind of perennial fountain of youth.

Yogi had originally filled the third segment of *The Huckleberry Hound Show*. From the enthusiastic way viewers responded to the wisecracking con artist, it was almost immediately apparent that he inevitably take center stage with a show of his own, which he did in 1960. Co-starring with Yogi was his admiring half-pint sidekick, Boo Boo, who despite Yogi's often outrageous rascality never wavered in his loyalty for the big guy.

The relationships that you build between characters are a critical factor in helping to define their individual personalities. This was true for Yogi and Boo Boo. Such interplay was an important element that remained constant throughout all the team scenarios of our characters. Joe has often described Boo Boo as being Yogi's conscience. As an incorrigible filcher of picnic baskets, Yogi was constantly hatching new schemes to enrich his larder often to little Boo Boo's dismay. The following exchange between the bear buddies might have a familiar ring to readers:

Boo Boo: "The Ranger's not going to like this, Yogi."
Yogi: "Hey-Hey! What the Ranger doesn't know isn't going to hurt him, little pal of mine!"

Yogi was always a great one for the snappy line and the blithe rhymed couplet that he would deliver with all the exuberance of an entrepreneur innocently convinced that he is a legend in his own mind. I've been told that Yogi's jaunty, effusive inflections are possibly the most imitated of all our characters. I can certainly believe it, for Daws Butler's voicing of Yogi was as classic an example of verbal characterization as any I've ever heard, and provided a perfect counterpoint to Don Messick's mild-mannered and self-effacing rendering of Boo Boo.

The visual environment of a cartoon is also a key ingredient used in establishing character identity. *Where* the characters are set suggests a great deal of *who* they are. In order to give Yogi and Boo Boo enough room to roam, we decided to come up with a whole national park called "Jellystone" which Yogi could claim as his own domain. Under the conscientious management of Ranger Smith (also voiced by Don Messick), Jellystone Park was a kind of tourist Eden. In essence, the park was a protected, pastoral preserve that underlined the essential innocence of our characters who, despite Yogi's hot-shot vanity, were actually quite unworldly.

By 1960, Hanna-Barbera Productions had nine shows in syndication and had become the dominant cartoon studio in the television industry, eclipsing even Walt Disney in production. A cursory look at a list of our shows at that time, which included *The Huckleberry Hound Show*, *Quick Draw McGraw*, *Yakky Doodle*, and *Yogi Bear*, would also seem to indicate that we had assembled the largest menagerie of cartoon stars as well.

With all due respect to Lassie, I do believe that the critters featured in our cartoons at Hanna-Barbera were among the most highly evolved animals on television. After all, we had dogs, cats, and bears that not only conversed fluently with people, but carried cash, credit cards, and drove cars as well.

As time marched on, however, it seemed inevitable that we evolve a cast of humans to star in a cartoon series. Real people! Human beings appearing at the dawn of an era—our vast three-year history thus far at Hanna-Barbera.

It would be a major milestone and it might have a rocky start. Hopefully, however, the new cast and their series would find their own place in history.

Chapter Ten

Cave Clan Culture

John Mitchell's telephone calls always seemed to have a familiar ring to them. Since Joe handled the sales end of our business, Mitchell's calls were generally directed to his side of our office. Knowing John, however, it wasn't difficult to guess the general thread of their conversations. It was Mitchell's zeal for our cartoon products that had in great part brought our campaign to dominate the TV animation market to full boil.

Joe had proven to be an able ally of Mitchell's. During the first two years following the formation of our company, my partner had generated an impressive volume of sales of shows to sponsors for the network and for syndication throughout the country. Together their promotional and sales drive had increased our production rate nearly tenfold over what we had done during our eighteen years at MGM. Hanna-Barbera had struck a bonanza with television, sure enough, but as it turned out Mitchell apparently had new designs on a different mother lode.

One afternoon, upon returning to our office from lunch, I found my partner pensive with excitement. I sensed his mood immediately. "What's up?" I asked without preamble. Joe had apparently been sketching through the noon hour with energetic abandon, a sure sign of his restless abstraction.

He tapped his pencil on the desk several times and coughed. "Bill, we had a call from Mitchell again. He's on fire with this idea of us trying to get one of our shows on primetime!"

I could tell by one look at Joe that he was sold on the idea. For that matter, so was I. Taking the leap from Saturday morning and suppertime shows to primetime broadcasts implied a dizzying advancement of the commercial respectability of animated entertainment on television.

Traditionally, the cartoon has generally been regarded as the stepchild of live-action motion pictures. This attitude had inevitably carried over into television as well. Cartoons were kiddie fare, and you simply did not run those shows along with a primetime lineup of adult programs.

The answer to such a sanction was very clear to both of us. Why not produce a half-hour animated program that would appeal to *adults* as well as children? The trick, of course, was to come up with a format that would hold its own among all the entrenched live-action programs against which we'd have to compete. As cartoon producers, Joe and I had often relied heavily on the creative principle that "art imitates life" to provide us with many of the gags and story situations in our films.

In gauging our prospects for competing in primetime TV, however, we switched tactics and revised the adage a bit. Animation would have to imitate live-action story concepts. If a half-hour animation show was to have a fighting chance to appeal to the older primetime viewers, we would have to take much of the adult humor currently being viewed and make it "cartoon friendly." Since situation comedy involving American suburban family life had proven to be popular and durable program fare, Joe and a team of our writers decided to develop a similar concept for a half-hour cartoon show.

Everyone at our studio seemed excited over the project. It implied definite opportunities to initiate some intriguing creative precedents, the most noteworthy perhaps being the introduction of our first principal cast of humans. Yes, folks, after twenty years as partners, Bill and Joe were embarking upon the production of their first cartoon show featuring honest-to-goodness people!

With all due respect to our little animated company of animals, nothing less than real two-legged folks would do for primetime. Congenial as critters could be, we would have to pass on packs, prides, litters, or herds and produce a genuinely wholesome yet refreshingly original human family for our nighttime viewers.

A quick look at the television neighborhood we were planning to crash revealed an assembly of wholesome families that would have been the pride of any PTA. The networks seemed to have settled into heartland America with such programs as *Father Knows Best, Leave It To*

Beaver, and *The Donna Reed Show*. It was real-meat-and potato-fare and the menu seemed to be selling, for these were all top-rated shows.

Well, if we couldn't beat 'em, Joe and I would join them—sort of, anyway. In conversations over coffee and more potent potables, my partner and I concluded that we'd have to come up with something more than a cartoon carbon copy version of one of these contemporary shows. We'd serve up the wholesome fare all right, but rather than dishing up roast beef, we might barbecue the meat a little.

Novelty is a magic word in the animation business, and we wanted to make our first primetime entry nothing short of magical. That was the task and, truth to tell, I would have to leave most of the conjuring of the storytelling magic to Joe and our writers.

As enthusiastic as we all were at gearing up for primetime programming, blazing a trail into this province was only one on a crowded list of priorities. We had other cartoon concepts to sell for Saturday morning broadcasts, and those that were sold and developed had to be produced while fulfilling our primetime aspirations.

Somehow it would be done. I could tell that Joe and some of our best writers, like Dan Gordon, Mike Maltese, Charlie Shows, and Warren Foster, all had their blood up for the challenge. Thank God, for our production schedule was, if anything, more vigorous than ever. Joe was acquiring a lot of air time of a different sort, flying back and forth from L.A. to New York pitching our shows to television executives. In addition, he was busier than ever working on story developments for all of our existing shows, including Huckleberry, Quick Draw, and the rest.

At the same time, I was entirely immersed in the production of these shows, a job that consumed an average of twelve hours a day, numerous club sandwiches, and at least a quart of black coffee. During the course of an average workday, my partner and I were always hastening toward our respective departments and duties, making time together more valuable. Although the days when Joe and I would leisurely sit opposite each other at a desk and brainstorm ideas were fast coming to an end, we continued to confer closely together on every aspect of company business. Along with the myriad other production concerns, Joe kept me constantly apprised of the creative development of our primetime entry.

Apparently conceptualizing a cartoon family that promised primetime panache had evolved into a real-trial-and-error process. The inescapable success quotient for situation comedies, whether they be live action or animated, is the freshness and humorous sparkle of the situation. We needed to give a new spin to our cartoon kin, but how? In their quest for originality, Joe and our writers had conjured all over the globe and eventually even back and forth through time.

The variety and volume of conceptual sketches and renderings considered for our new primetime clan would normally have provided enough developmental art for five or six cartoon shows. I was amazed at the amount of graphite spent and the countless hours of discussion consumed in an effort to calculate the appeal various characters might have for our viewers. We were throwing a wide net.

For weeks there were avid discussions suggesting that the characters be made in a whole variety of ways. They were designed as Indians, as Gypsies, even as Pilgrims. No one was really thrilled by any of it. The sparks weren't flying. What was missing? Were we being overly critical? Maybe we were all merely suffering from a bad case of performance anxiety over being pushed into the high stakes arena of nighttime television.

It was an addictive puzzle. The damned thing had a way of growing on you, and what's more there was a hell of a lot of money riding on making the right choices. Just about the time when all of these conferences appeared to be reaching critical mass, Dan Gordon dashed off a little sketch that jump-started the whole endeavor and set it humming with new excitement.

The drawing depicted two characters dressed in caveman skins along with a primitive phonograph that consisted of a little bird with a sharp beak on a stone record. It was an historic moment, or rather more precisely a prehistoric one. When we saw Dan's drawing, I think we all recognized the gag potential of a cartoon show that burlesqued modern conveniences (as we knew them in 1960) and adapting them to the Stone Age.

From that point on, "everyone," as Jimmy Durante was fond of asserting, "wanted to get into the act." Dan's clever little sketch opened a whole new region of cartoon comedy that invited the creation of fanciful humorous parallels drawn between cultures centuries apart, yet timeless in their common human dilemmas.

As a result, we came up with some wonderful gags, like the mastodon with a trunk that the characters used as a hose to take a shower or wash the car. Some of my personal favorites worked up for the show included gags depicting a little bird stationed at the Flintstone's door that served as a doorbell, and a warthog assigned to duty under the sink as a garbage disposal.

With a wellspring of original gimmicks and gags assured, the rest of the format for the show just seemed to fall into place. Sight gags playing off the prehistoric concept naturally led to a rich potential of puns and phrases for dialogue playing off the whole Stone Age angle.

Story conferences discussing various elements of the show, including gadgets, character names, and place names, spawned a whole series of quips and word plays. The Stone Age community in which the show would be set was designated as the town of Bedrock, located in the seat of Cobblestone County.

This was a show we were definitely taking for granite! Please don't wince—that was the kind of unabashed Neanderthal humor that we were sure would put that show on solid ground. Consistent with the show's theme, all of the surnames of the projected characters would have identities indicating a geological origin. Names like Rockpile, Stonewall, and Quartz were among the obvious offerings suggestive of our caveman theme. Especially critical was the sculpting of the personalities of our main characters and digging up names for them worthy of being written in stone.

The show would focus on the relationship between two neighboring suburban couples. The characters slated to receive top billing were a blustery blue-collar kind of a guy named Fred Flagstone who worked in a rock quarry and his tender-hearted, but somewhat tart-tongued, common-sense wife, Wilma.

There is an old saying that admonishes: "He who fails to learn from history is fated to repeat it." Sound advice, but the implicit challenge before us in conceptualizing this new show demanded that we take our lessons from the present in order to rewrite the past.

Cavemen and women would never have it so good. Never mind the raw meat, bleak wilderness, primitive dens, and savage struggle for survival that had been the grim lot of primitive man as related in textbooks and anthropological quarterlies. Our guys and gals would be clad in animal skins, but they would also share a congenial cave clan culture with all of its semi-savage if not civilized amenities.

Give or take a few centuries, our Bedrock folks would be as comfortably middle-class as anyone living in Springfield, or Riverdale, USA. They would have cars and comfortable tract housing, or rather caving, and drive-in restaurants. More significantly, however, our characters would share relationships that mirrored many of our contemporary social values and attitudes—all in a spirit of fun, of course.

Both Joe and I knew that if our cartoon plots were to play well to older viewers, they would have to have more of a sophisticated edge to them than the cute Saturday morning fare we'd been doing thus far. The humor would need a wit that adults could both identify with and relate to with laughter. That meant a lot of spoofs in the comedy, and the elements that seemed to naturally invite the most parody at the time were those relating to modern marriage and home life.

Since neither Joe's schedule nor my own allowed for a lot of time to watch television, we were not the best authorities on how this subject matter was treated on TV season to season. We knew that in general, most family shows were pretty idealized and depicted different couples who seemed to abide in domestic bliss within an idyllic, elm-tree-shaded suburbia. From what I can recall of my sporadic TV viewing in those days, many of these folks seemed to be indefatigably loving and patient with each other and as well-adjusted as the fine tuned image on the TV sets.

Despite its doubtless and durable appeal, that sort of take on family life seemed a trifle tame for the needs of a thirty-minute cartoon show. What we wanted to work up was a perspective on married life that was saltier, somewhat irreverent, and possessed of enough oomph and open zaniness to take fullest advantage of the show's rich gag potential.

Was there anything like that around on the air at the time? Indeed there was; a kind of anomaly, in fact, among family shows called *The Honeymooners*. I personally thought that *The Honeymooners* was the funniest half-hour on television. That was undoubtedly a biased conclusion, for it was just about the *only* half-hour of entertainment I watched on TV in those days. It was enough, however, to convince me that the format for this Jackie Gleason sitcom contained some inspiring elements for our own upcoming offering of primetime comedy.

Here was a show that really played it for laughs. Instead of portraying the conventional romantic couple, Ralph and Alice Kramden were cast as a flippant and fractious bickering pair who waged a kind of guerrilla war between the sexes. As a viewer, you were caught in the crossfire every week as Ralph and Alice exchanged barbs in an ongoing marital rivalry of one-upmanship. Now here was a real relationship!

The Honeymooners presented viewers with a refreshingly realistic take on marriage, presenting a relationship with all the warts that a mainstream audience could personally identify with. What's more, the show possessed a broad and campy hilarity that really set me on my heels. My partner pretty much felt the same way. Slapstick humor appealed to him as much as it did to me. He had often drawn from a great store of personal knowledge of the distinct comedy styles of Chaplin, Abbott and Costello, and other classic clown princes of the genre for inspiration in his own writing.

Well, if we could chew the scenery with shows like *The*

Honeymooners in primetime, we would be in good comedic company. As impressed with the show as both Joe and I were, it was perhaps inevitable that many of the humorous elements of the Gleason comedy ended up having a singular creative impact on our cartoon show.

Turning out the primetime show required that we retool a lot of our production methods. This involved in particular a different division of labor. Heretofore, all of our production had been directed toward turning out the cartoon "variety" shows which combined individual seven-minute cartoons to fill the half-hour segments. Everyone worked on everything and that was fine.

In addressing the demands of producing a single half-hour cartoon, however, it was necessary to assign a special corps of writers, artists, animators, and other personnel to work specifically on the primetime show. Our seventeen-year run of producing Tom and Jerry had taught Joe and me the value of maintaining an overall aligned team effort in crafting a show that would throb with consistent creativity.

It had proved to be a good system, and it seemed to be working for *The Flagstones*. Everyone was starting to get in sync with the emerging spirit of the show and getting a feel for the developing concept. Spirits soared with optimism as the show's release date grew nearer. Our primetime premiere would be primitive but prestigious. The initial character sketches drawn by Dan Gordon had evolved into some wonderful Stone Age characters developed on wonderful model sheets by another of our staff, Ed Benedict.

Enthusiasm was running high, and then suddenly all of that enthusiasm turned into high anxiety as we hit an unexpected bump. The news came to me in a brief, dismal phone call one morning from Joe. "Bill," he said, "we're looking at a possible law suit." I was stunned. "What the hell for?" I demanded, aghast. "There's a row over the name of our cartoon, *The Flagstones*. It turns out that it happens to be the last name for a family of comic strip characters named "Hi and Lois."

Our Stone Age family was having an identity crisis. We would have to rename them or get sued. With deep regrets we reluctantly bid adieu to *The Flagstones*, and commenced a search for another prehistoric handle. It was too bad. We had sincerely believed that the Flagstones was a refreshingly original name, and as it turned out it was—only not for us.

A frustrating trial-and-error process followed, involving numerous lackluster suggestions like "The Gladstones." I was never thrilled by that one, although temporarily failing anything else more appealing, we used it temporarily as an identification for the artistic development of the characters on many of our model sheets. Finally someone, I don't recall exactly who, came up with a name that instantly struck a distinct spark: *The Flintstones.*

That earlier bump in the road regarding the Flagstones had turned us onto a fortunate detour. Our primitive primetime entry was happily re-christened *The Flintstones*, a name so appropriate to the show's character that today I can't imagine that it could have ever been called anything else.

You can call it intuition or just reckless wishful thinking, but I had a persistent notion that somehow this show would really make a name for itself. The team had produced something extraordinary. I could feel it in my gut. All of the wide-open gag appeal, slapstick humor, and irreverent wit potential so evident in the show's concept had developed astonishingly well, I thought, and were richly apparent in the very first scripts and storyboards. As much as I loved all of our previous cartoon shows, they had all been done for children, and all of our creative efforts had been accordingly constrained to producing a kind of naive and ingenuous humor for our viewers.

The Flintstones would be primarily for, well, bigger kids, like ourselves in the animation business, mischievous grownups who had in reality never become completely adult.

Casting the voice talent for *The Flintstones* was yet another undertaking that brought its own share of mishaps. The initial selection of Jean Vander Pyl and Bea Benaderet to provide the voices of Betty Rubble and Wilma Flintstone proved to be a wonderful alignment, and their performances sparkled from the first auditions. But it was a considerably rockier road to find the right guys to do Fred and Barney. The actors first selected for the roles proved to be dismally miscast and had to be replaced at the cost of a considerably expensive settlement.

Fortunately, this made way for the recruitment of two veteran talents, Alan Reed and Mel Blanc, who respectively breathed vocal life into Fred Flintstone and Barney Rubble that seemed inspired by the cartoon gods themselves.

We had (with apologies for the adjectives) a rock-solid cast that formed a firm character foundation for the show. As the series developed this host of talent went on to welcome some sparkling guest stars, including occasional celebrities such as Tony Curtis and Elizabeth Montgomery, who provided the voices for their animated Stone Age cartoon counterparts. One of my favorite episodes in this genre featured lovely Ann-Margret cast as the glamorous singer "Ann-Margrock."

The story called for Ann-Margret's character to appear incognito as a babysitter for the Flintstones after little Pebbles takes a shine to her. Included in the episode is a fantasy dream sequence that showcased Ann-Margret's exquisite singing of a tender lullaby that to this day brings a tear to my eye.

Ann-Margret's brilliant career, of course, is one of the great success stories in the entertainment industry, and I'm proud to chronicle her performance as "Ann-Margrock" here as a Flintstone classic. She was kind enough to phone me recently and share a few memories of that time—and boy, I'll tell you, that brightened my morning!

To my delight, I learned from her that our Stone Age singing sensation has become a perennial element of Ann-Margret's own glamorous identity. "It was such a fun show, Bill," she recalled. "They showed me the character, which was three-quarters fluffy bright red hair, and I thought she was absolutely adorable.

"In one wonderful way the fun has never stopped. Believe it or not, to this day little children who really don't know that I'm an actress will come up to me and ask, 'Are you Ann-Margrock?'"

What's in a name? Well, in this happy recollection, it is the ageless appeal of a winsome character imparted by a timeless talent.

In addition to coordinating the creative development of *The Flintstones*, Joe had done a yeoman's job of pitching and selling the show to the network. After a grueling several weeks flying back and forth from Los Angeles to New York armed with storyboards from our first two episodes, Joe pulled off the coup of selling the program to ABC, then obtained two major sponsors for the show as well.

With the dawn about to rise upon our cave clan civilization, I embarked upon the eager task of working up a main title theme song that would really give the show some rousing wake-up music. In this I was aided by our musical director, Hoyt Curtin, whose ability to create a bright and lilting melody to match my lyrics was to me nothing short of astonishing. Hoyt is a prolific composer with a passion for jazz possessed of a kind of genteel classiness that he shares with Henry Mancini and Burt Bacharach.

Hoyt and I had collaborated on most of the main title themes for our cartoon shows, and the majority of them had been done under the most informal circumstances. I would generally compose the lyrics in my head, jot them down on a sheet of note paper, give Hoyt a call at his home, and recite them over the telephone. Almost invariably, Hoyt would call me back within a day or so with a musical composition and sing the thing to me complete with my lyrics.

That was pretty much the way we came up with the words and music for *The Flintstones'* main theme song, although there were two things that occurred during the composition that were a little out of the ordinary. The first was that most of the songs that Hoyt and I wrote followed a creative sequence in which I would write the lyrics first and Hoyt would generally compose music to fit the words. While working on *The Flintstones* however, we did just the reverse and I had to come up with a pattern of words and meter to fit the beat of Hoyt's little melody.

The other thing was the inclusion of a little word invention that was improvised by Alan Reed while recording one of the earliest shows. To the best of my recollection, Joe was up in the booth directing the recording. Alan had a script in his hand and noticed that a line called for him to shout, "Yahoo!" This had been done a couple of times in the first show, but Alan came up with something that he thought had a better ring to it.

"Hey Joe!" boomed Alan in his now famous stentorian Flintstone voice. "Do you mind if I say 'Yabba-Dabba-Doo'?" Joe shrugged and nodded in assent. The word stayed in the script and stuck in my mind. Recalling it while writing the main title lyrics, I decided to put it into the song.

Main title themes are generally straightforward little songs that are meant to introduce a cartoon show to the audience with a few catchy words that suggest the personalities and general situation of the characters involved. This is presented through a kind of "mini-cartoon" that runs about ninety seconds and serves as a preview to the main cartoon itself.

These little pictures, along with a similar closing animated segment displaying the credits that generally runs about thirty seconds, combine in essence, to become the trademark of the cartoon show. As a condensed visual representative of the show, these clips should possess, I've always felt, a definite panache of their own. Although by this time I generally deferred the job of devising gags for the shows to our writers, I still occasionally enjoyed providing a hands-on contribution along these lines when the spirit moved me. During the course of directing the animation for *The Flintstones* title and credits, I felt that it was important to feature up front a couple of Stone Age gags for the viewers to keep them tuned in for the main event, as well as include something in the credits to leave 'em laughing.

The Flintstones opens and closes with our main characters heading off to, and coming home from, a night out at a drive-in movie. On their return in the credits segment, I thought it would be a cute idea to have the family stop at a drive-in restaurant and literally "flip out." Timing the amount of frames I knew were allotted in this ninety-second run, I made some notes on Hoyt's music sheets that worked in a little gag where the waitress staggers over with a huge serving tray that she places on the side of the Flintstones' car. To the dismay of the family, the weight of the thing topples the car over to one side. The mishap itself I thought offered a nice slapstick balance to what would become a weekly comedic wrapper for the show.

For some reason, the lyrics of *The Flintstones'* theme song—in typical 1960s fashion, pretty upbeat—seem to have become the most recognizable words of any of our cartoon theme songs. It's a mystery to me as to exactly why, but I imagine that a big part of it certainly has to do with Hoyt's bright melody with its distinctive octave leap that really made the thing stick in your ear.

For a number of years these *Flintstone* lyrics created for several viewers a kind of persistent riddle. I can recall folks coming up to me and asserting that they could make out most of the words when listening to the song on TV but were unsure of what one particular phrase actually said. "What?" I was invariably asked, "were the words that ended the phrase beginning with 'through the courtesy of Fred's—?'"

Well, in answer to the one and only trivia quiz offered in this book, I set down for the record the complete set of lyrics for *The Flintstones*.

> Flint-stones—Meet the Flint-stones
> They're a modern stone age fam-i-ly
> From the—town of Bed-rock
> They're a page right out of his-to-ry
> Let's ride—with the family down the street
> Through the—cour-te-sy of Fred's two feet
> When you're—with the Flintstones
> Have a yabba dabba doo time
> A dabba doo time
> We'll have a great—old—time!

The Flintstones premiered on ABC on September 30, 1960. The initial reviews were far from laudatory. Critic Jack Gould, writing in the October 1 issue of the *New Yorker*, dismissed the show as "an inked disaster" and went on to describe our male characters as being "coarse and gruff" and the women "nondescript."

Both Joe and I had developed thick skins regarding that sort of criticism. Anyone involved in the cartoon business, or for that matter in television itself, absolutely had to work something out in their egos that enabled them to deal with rejection, censure, or even open ridicule. The folks that we really wanted to hear from were that silent majority called the viewers, who spoke to us by either tuning in or tuning out.

As it turned out, the audience elected to tune in—and as the ratings climbed, the critics' tone began to change. By the third season we were in apparent good favor with reviewers in general. Although I seldom had the time or inclination to wade through critiques of our shows, I do remember seeing some clippings that referred to each weekly *Flintstones* episode as a "remarkably fresh cartoon."

Well, that was our *raison d'etre* in a nutshell. Succinctly put, producing "a remarkably fresh cartoon" was why we were all in business.

A lot of the show's hilarity, I think, can be credited to the apparent sly innocence with which the characters employ one gimmick after another, playing off the whole "Stone Age counterpart to modern lifestyle" theme. Fred's use of a clam shell with a buzzing bee in it as a shaver or Wilma cleaning house with the trunk of a baby mastodon as the hose of a vacuum cleaner seemed to be the most natural of everyday functions for our Neolithic neighbors.

One of the most enduring elements of good comedy, I believe, is the open display of clever gags employed by characters who are apparently oblivious to their humorous implication. Fred, Wilma, Barney, and Betty all played the Stone Age gimmicks for laughs, but they generally did it with straight faces that were often so dead pan that they would have made Buster Keaton proud.

At any rate, that's part of my theory as to why this "modern Stone Age family" and their pals have not yet been relegated to a museum. Maybe I'm right, because although nearly four decades have passed since *The Flintstones* premiered, new generations of viewers still seem to enjoy riding "with the family down the street, through the courtesy of Fred's two feet."

Chapter Eleven

Studio Portrait

ad I been inclined to such things, the year 1960 would have provided me with occasion to celebrate a thirty-year anniversary in the animation business. In July of that same year, I turned fifty. Such milestones might beg a tempting question: Was I confronted at the same time with a mid-life crisis? Quite frankly, no, although I might just be getting around to that now.

During the fledgling years of our little company of Hanna-Barbera Productions, both my partner (who is about a year younger than I) and myself shared a kind of freshman's eagerness for the advancement of our enterprise, as well as a confident excitement regarding its prospects for growth. Although my prematurely white hair might seem to belie this assertion, I believe it to be essentially true that the cartoon business helps keep you young. Our professional existence, in essence, is devoted toward either turning out a product for our kids, or turning out a product that can still beguile the kid in all of us.

In short, there seems to be a kind of prevailing "animation attitude" that fosters our perennial fascination for fun. For most of us who make cartoons the mystery of life's motion is magical. Fortunately for Bill and Joe, the overall movement of our company's life during those first few years of its inception had been fast and frantically forward. By 1960, the rapidly accelerating production demands of turning out a primetime series as well as ten other cartoon shows literally had our outfit bursting at the seams. The dynamism of entrepreneurial events may have helped me elude a mid-life crisis, but it also produced professional growing pains for both my partner and myself.

It was time not only to move on but to move out. During the first few years that we had been situated at the Chaplin studio, Joe and I had continued to provide facilities for our growing staff by renting offices throughout the Hollywood area and converting them into work studios. We also continued to subcontract the camera and recording work, since the purchase of such equipment represented a hefty expenditure of capital for a company still struggling to stay under the frugal production budgets allocated by our agency clients.

All well and good, but it was becoming increasingly apparent that we could no longer afford to indulge in such expediency if we wished to efficiently continue to meet our growing contractual demands. The time had come to centralize both our staff and personnel, as well as all of our production facilities, into a single location. Hanna-Barbera Productions was coming of age and required the creation of its own independent cartoon studio.

But where? Actually, the answer came easily enough and without a whole lot of canvassing. While scouting for likely sites during the early months of 1961, I noticed a four acre tract of vacant land in Hollywood along Cahuenga Boulevard, situated next to a monkey farm and a tiny amusement park featuring children's pony rides. I had come to know this area fairly well over the years. As a kid, I had camped with my Boy Scout troop at a wooded facility just about a mile or two east down the road. When Cahuenga Pass was later paved into Cahuenga Boulevard, I had driven the route many times to work in Hollywood.

Allowing for the increase in automobile traffic and the construction of a few additional homes and a mom-and-pop market or two, the area hadn't really changed that much. The lot I had my eye on was still covered with grass and completely undeveloped. It seemed to have just about the right acreage necessary for us to build on. After conferring with Joe, who came out to look the site over, we decided to contact the real estate office and make an offer.

Such a deal! Looking back now over a span of more than thirty years, the initial purchase price we paid for the land was a thumping bargain. That is, of course, a perspective offered after three and a half decades of capital gain. At the time we signed the papers, however, my partner and I both had to take a long hard swallow to extend the dearly earned cash.

While we folded our tents and prepared to vacate the Chaplin lot, Joe and I discussed plans for the new studio's construction with the building contractor we'd engaged, and outlined the various departments we planned to have on the premises. The rudimentary layout followed the basic design of our old animation studio at MGM. Our dominant priority was to create an entirely self-contained cartoon studio that would possess all of the facilities necessary for production and business development.

Fundamentally, we would require office space to accommodate departments for writers, storyboard artists, layout people and designers, animators, checkers, a color model unit, inkers and painters, and editors and movieolas. Just as critical was the inclusion of a recording studio and camera department that would enable us to handle that end of production in-house, rather than to continue relying on subcontractors.

Since it was estimated that construction of the studio would not be completed for more than a year, it was necessary to occupy some tentative facilities for the duration. Luckily we were able to rent an office building on Cahuenga about two blocks away from our own property. The place was an unglamorous, single-story cigar box of a building, but it was large enough to house a main portion of our personnel. Shortly after signing a short-term lease on the place, we folded our tents and vacated the Chaplin Studio.

My daughter, Bonnie, who was about twenty then and working as a painter, cheerfully remembers that the temporary place was utterly barren of windows and natural sunlight. "I loved working for you in those days, Dad," she recently recalled, "but I never knew whether it was day or night working with those fluorescent lights in our room." Despite such definite drawbacks, the place allowed both Joe and me to retain individual offices and to subdivide the floorspace to provide enough work areas for the primary production units.

It was admittedly a little cramped, but I was tremendously excited by this primary move to gather all our people from the diverse sub-studios scattered around town and to centralize them in one location. Along with the obvious logistical advantages, such unity was good for morale. Both Joe and I believed that the excitement and efficiency of these creatively diverse people working together in cartoon production would be greatly enhanced when they felt a part of the whole cohesive process. In addition to their involvement with the mechanics of turning out individual cartoon programs, these folks, many of them veteran colleagues, had become members of our company family. They were all in essence talented stars in their own right and part of a cast of friends enrolled at Hanna-Barbera Productions.

For the next several months, as the bulldozers plowed just down the street and the skeleton frame of a two-story structure began to sprout, those of us in the windowless building on Cahuenga carried on, thoroughly absorbed in our own fluorescent world of frenzied production activity. During breaks and on our lunch hours, we would escape outdoors to be startled by the sunlight and to temporarily reacquaint ourselves with a larger world beyond storyboards and exposure sheets.

Occasionally I'd succumb to the temptation of wandering down the street to watch the progress of the construction. There was something about the screech of the power saws, the smell of the fresh-cut lumber, and the pounding of all those nails that used to stir something right in the pit of my stomach. It was a strange mixture of the undeniable excitement of witnessing the birth of our own studio, and a kind of nostalgia that hearkened back to my own experiences working on the construction scaffolding at the Pantages Theatre.

That one-story fall which had put me in the hospital over thirty years earlier had turned out to be one of the luckiest breaks in my life. Well, here I was, still in one piece and watching a structure take shape before my eyes that would become a place no less dearer than home itself to me. I can recall interviewers who have referred to the interim time of our studio's construction as a "period of transition." Well, hell, looking back then, as I do now, it seemed that my whole career from that first day of work at Harman-Ising had involved a whole *series* of periods of transition.

Flush times, lean times, down time, vicissitudes of all sorts are the lot of anyone in this business. And yet, as chaotic as they often seemed at the time, there were periods of retrospection such as the ones I enjoyed while watching our Cahuenga studio blossom—when the changes, whatever they were, seemed to form a pattern amazing in its perfection.

In other words, things had worked out. Joe and I had been lucky, but we had also worked our tails off as well and taken some big chances. During the busy years following the close of MGM and the formation of our own company, both of us had constantly striven to make time for our families despite the rigorous hours we were putting in. My own two kids, David and Bonnie, had grown up during the fifties and had both entered college by the time Fred Flintstone let loose with his first "yabba dabba doo" yell.

They had been crowded years, but full ones as well for the family. Despite the inevitable tense times of adolescent rebelliousness or parental bewilderment, somehow we had all worked together to make the time to be together. David and I had shared scouting activities and then, of course, like most teenagers, he had gone to share activities with other friends just as I once had. Although he labored through his own share of sibling rivalry with his sister, David had remained close pals with Bonnie throughout their childhood. Bonnie still remembers how David was determined to teach his baby sister certain skills that he believed were absolutely essential to master, like how to burn rubber on all four wheels in the family car.

Both of my kids have denied to me that they felt particularly deprived or neglected by me during those first years of the company, when my work schedule consumed twelve or fourteen hours a day. Admittedly, I think a large part of this was due to the fact that both my children were already in their late teens and were young adults exploring lives of their own by then. Unlike the analytical era of today (which has its merits), neither Vi nor I tried to be very psychological in bringing up our kids. We relied primarily on common sense, the trial-and-error process, and the golden rule for the basic ethics of parenthood—along with an unsparing resource of love. Vi and I had our reward in the realization that our kids were growing up but not away from us. We had all remained close as a family, but we had all somehow instinctively given each other room to grow.

David had enrolled as a business administration major at the University of Arizona and was generally only able to get home on holidays. Despite his childhood bout with rheumatic fever, he had grown into a robust and aggressive young guy endowed with an optimistic self-confidence that often astonished me. David had drive, and even in those freshman years displayed an entrepreneurial audacity that seemed to me to augur some prodigious success. I was as proud as hell of him and would indulge myself in a bit of gruff paternal crowing with such remarks as, "My son's got more guts than a slaughterhouse."

Bonnie had entered the University of Southern California and usually visited us at the house every weekend. I had always been somewhat more protective of Bonnie than David through her childhood. I imagine that a lot of it might have had to do with the chronic kidney problems and the persistent suffering I knew it often caused her. Part of it also, I'm sure, was simply because she was always my little girl and a game one at that, whose shy, sensitive spirit was never permanently maimed by severely curtailed childhood activities, illness, or embarrassment.

Bonnie was a lot like her old man in the sense that she seemed to be primarily a kind of blue-collar worker at heart. I'd spent a lot of good times during my boyhood working alongside my own dad in his construction crews, and Bonnie appeared to have inherited that same affection for sharing manual labor—with me at least. We worked together on carpentry or painting projects in our garage on weekends.

I must admit that in this case the temptation of cheap labor (she could usually be bought off with an orange soda and corned beef sandwich) proved too great for me. Bonnie became my "gopher" and proved to be an indispensable adjutant. She learned to operate a paint spray gun with the dexterity of a journeyman and knew her way unerringly around a toolbox.

In all fairness, much of this natural resourcefulness must have been in the genes and a direct inheritance from Violet, who generally approved of our woodworking sessions, although she occasionally looked reproachfully at me when she noticed Bonnie's fingernails.

In one significant way the manicurist's loss was ultimately a gain for Hanna-Barbera. Consistent with what we considered to be the artistic and enterprising spirit of our company, I decided that our work community should become a "do it yourself studio" as much as possible. This was consistent with the spirit of the industry that I grew up with.

People in the cartoon business have traditionally always had a kind of arts-and-crafts attitude regarding the design of their individual work environments. Artists, animators, inkers, and painters instinctively personalize their offices, rooms, or whatever kind of unit made available to them. They proudly adorn their desks, walls, and doors with snapshots of family or fellow co-workers, whimsical hand-lettered posters, humorous signs, and other forms of individual artwork and personal projects.

In addition, many veterans are fond of devising ingenious little gadgets or tools designed to aid or to expedite their work in some little way appropriate to their own individual style or method of operation. The phrase, "Necessity is the mother of invention," was never more vividly demonstrated than in the homemade environment of a cartoon studio.

One of my best film editors and oldest friends, Pat Foley, still has in his office a simple little device of four pieces of metal welded together as a sort of hanging rack with a base, featuring little hooks from which loops of common thread wire are suspended, that he uses to hang strips of film in orderly sequence.

Consistent with this spirit of American ingenuity, I decided with my daughter's assistance to make our own contribution to providing the studio with some customized animation desks. After purchasing the necessary lumber, I set up a wood shop in my garage. We spent several Saturdays working with my power tools to build several of the desks for our artists, animators, and ink and paint people, complete with ample shelf and drawer space.

Bonnie, as always, proved to be an able aide-de-camp and stood ready to bring me all of the necessary tools with the earnest efficiency of a nurse assisting a surgeon. When the desks were constructed, it was Bonnie who applied the finishing touch of a lavish coat of brown-speckled zolotone paint on the furniture with a paint gun connected to an air compressor. (There's one still around today.)

We were like a large clan waiting to move from the tenements into "the big house." By early spring of 1963, the main two-story building had been erected and the dry walls applied. During the final weeks of the studio's completion, I think just about every member of our company must have taken frequent field trips on their breaks or after work and eagerly walked down the street to visit the construction site. Some of the kids seemed nearly inclined to camp out and work in the place even before the lights were turned on. One of our artists, Barbara Krueger, still wistfully recalls venturing down the vacant halls with pals like Allison Leopold from the ink and paint department, breathing the smell of fresh plaster and paint and dodging the scrap lumber and nickel slugs that were still strewn on the floor.

Joe was particularly elated over the ultra-modern beauty of the structure. He became a virtual volunteer tour guide, leading friends through the premises on weekend nights, pointing out with unabashed pride the building's sculpted latticework exterior, moat, fountains, and other elements of our virgin studio's architectural splendor.

Construction of the new Hanna-Barbera cartoon studio, located at 3400 Cahuenga Boulevard, was completed around the middle of 1963. Our occupation of the premises was pretty informal. It was certainly not a media event; there was not even, as I can recall, a ribbon-cutting ceremony of any sort. The excitement generated over the studio's opening was strictly a company affair, and our company was pretty much preoccupied with the practical logistics of moving furniture, equipment, art and office supplies, and personal belongings down the street, settling in, and doing it all without missing a production air date.

As far as the public was concerned, the team of Hanna-Barbera was far from being considered empire builders. We were still just a couple of guys who turned out television cartoons and had simply relocated in the process. In-house, however, it was a different matter. While there was no formal celebration, the feelings of festivity were in the air: many toasts were drunk in coffee with paper cups, and Baby Ruth candy bars and Laura Scudder's potato chips circulated freely.

My own daughter, Bonnie, was particularly elated for the most guileless reasons. After laboring for months in an artificially lit cavern, the abundant sunlit surroundings sent her into ecstasy. "I knew you and Joe Barbera had made it, Dad," she recently told me with characteristic candor, "when I walked into our new building and saw that we had windows!"

Following the studio's inauguration, the influx of new personnel resulting from our increased production demands quickly swelled the company ranks. By 1964, we had about 400 employees on board. In order to defray some of the studio's construction costs, we had initially decided to rent a portion of the second-floor offices to an engineering firm. That situation changed very quickly when we found ourselves once again confronted with a shortage of work space for our own people, and we subsequently reclaimed the entire second floor for the studio.

During the next few years, the studio expanded to include the construction of a two-story annex building, a warehouse, and eventually, an outdoor lunch and break area for employees and guests. Various production departments, such as the sound and editorial units, were shifted, gerrymandered, and relocated around the studio many times in order to accommodate the needs resulting from their constant technical development and increase in staff.

Pat Foley originally joined our company as a kid wiping cels, and shortly afterward went to work as a journeyman in the film editing department. He remembers that the company was originally equipped with eight movieolas, and the film editors assigned workspace in a northwest wing on the first floor. By early 1965, however, the volume of film requiring editing had increased so dramatically that we had to relocate the editing department in the studio's basement for several years in order to provide them with the necessary floor space.

The decade of the 1960s was, in essence, the salad years of Hanna-Barbera. Most of my old friends and veteran colleagues remember them as an incredibly fruitful period of television production. Considering the seasonal nature of this business, that was wonderfully gratifying to a bunch of kids who needed the money badly in order to make the rent and meet their car payments. But in recalling that period now over a span of more than three decades, it occurs to me that that era was also one of experimentation and innovation for everyone involved in the business.

The unassuming Huck and Quick Draw and Fred and Barney cartoons that blossomed from storyboards in color and form and distinct style on the work tables of our artists, inkers, painters and background people were the forerunners—the great granddaddies, if you will—of the immense panoply of sophisticated animation programs that fill our television airwaves today.

Over the years, Joe and I have received a lot of press and praise regarding our involvement in animation production. The real unsung pioneers of these endeavors, however, are the people who along with us in those early years devoted their energies to imparting the personal touches of creative inventiveness, as well as technical skill, in refining the methods and techniques of their profession. Cartoonmaking for our people was a craft, and few of us as craftspeople, I believe, ever gave much thought to the possibility that by unassumingly doing our jobs, we might also be developing a new industry.

The studio as it evolved then has apparently, I have often been told, become a kind of distinct landmark for this area of Hollywood. I suppose that's a great deal more preferable to it becoming a *landfill* of the region. At any rate, the place to me is home. It has taken on a life and character that has become inextricably woven into my own life, and I am sure, with that of my partner Joe.

Although there are several old friends who continue to work with us on the lot, and others who consistently visit, retirement, death, and the other varied and implacable summons of life have somewhat thinned the original ranks. After over thirty years, many of these folks have moved on, and their dispersal makes me protective of their legacy. Despite their absence, our studio remains energized, humorized, and humanized by the spirit of its people. There are days when I am not sure whether I haunt the beloved halls, or if they in truth haunt me.

Chapter Twelve

Commercial Breaks

The future looked bright to our growing company during the soaring sixties, and we ambitiously decided to share that vision with our television audience. During the crowded months of preparation for the great leap forward into our own studio, Joe and our writers were also busy with the development of a new cartoon series designed to propel viewers into the ultra-modern world of the twenty-first century. Encouraged by the growing popularity of *The Flintstones*, it seemed creatively logical to conceive a show calculated to transport our audience from the first frontier of the Stone Age to the final frontier of the Space Age.

Similar in format to *The Flintstones*, the new series would focus on the adventures of another typical suburban family—with one major difference. This new cartoon cast would be launched into a futuristic setting where they would literally become stars in their own inter-galactic society.

The Jetsons premiered on ABC in September 1962. The new show featured a well-rounded family who were introduced one by one in our main title song:

> Meet George Jetson
> Jane, his wife
> Daughter Judy
> His boy Elroy

In addition, the Jetson family unit included a rambunctious family dog named Astro. He was evolved enough in rover intellect to actually communicate in English with his owners, despite an inescapable tendency to begin every word with the letter "r"—"Rots of ruck!" (Astro's impertinent aptitude for speech would later be adapted for use by another cartoon canine with timid instincts and a ravenous appetite named Scooby Doo.) Completing the household was a robot with maternal instincts named Rosie who was the prototype of hired hardware help.

In general theme *The Jetsons* may appear to be the mere flip side of *The Flintstones*, but each series had quite a distinct look, tone, and feel of its own. The visual elements employed in *The Flintstones* were to look as solid in suggestion as the name of their hometown of Bedrock. The paints and colors used in the scenes were generally earthy and warm, and the artwork thick-textured and substantial. Boulders, caves, and primitive implements were all drawn in a manner calculated to project a massive and rounded physical impression of the Stone Age.

While *The Flintstones* were vividly earthy in appearance, *The Jetsons* series by contrast, was distinctly airy in its overall design. The characters and costumes, along with the vehicles, props, and structures of the show, were drawn in a streamlined mode distinctly suggestive of what our artists envisioned as being the look of the distant future.

In addition, the selection of colors used for the series appeared to come from an entirely different palate than those used in *The Flintstones*. Earth shades and pastoral hues were distinctly colors of the past. In their place our artists referred to a whole new spectrum of celestial blues, metallic grays, and synthetic pastels in order to impart distinctly modern tones to the computerized and climatized world of *The Jetsons*.

The one element in this series that was definitely not alien in principle to *The Flintstones*, nor any of our other shows for that matter, was the fine cast of voice talent assembled for the production. The late veteran actor George O'Hanlon provided the voice for George Jetson, and actress Penny Singleton, famed for her many film portrayals as "Blondie," was cast as the fetchingly futuristic wife, Jane. Daughter Judy was voiced by Janet Waldo, Daws Butler provided the pre-adolescent inflections of the Jetsons' son Elroy, and Jean Vander Pyl endowed the metallic Rosie, the Robot, with a transistorized irony all her own.

To our disappointment, however, although we were able to get *The Jetsons* off the launching pad, the series essentially failed to go into orbit in the primetime galaxy. Despite a great cast, the repletion of gags, gimmicks, and what seemed to us to be very clever and funny storylines, the ratings for *The Jetsons* seldom managed to climb as high as their family space vehicle.

In retrospect, there were probably several reasons why the series foundered at the time. Most obviously daunting was the fact that we were placed in a time slot opposite the formidable competition of two other established family shows, *Walt Disney's Wonderful World of Color* and *Dennis the Menace*.

Well, you can't win 'em all—right away, that is. Despite a game struggle to hold its own in a primetime slot, *The Jetsons* headed for an untimely splashdown at the end of the season. Joe attributes some of the show's early difficulties to an observation that despite the success of *The Flintstones*, adult television viewers may not have yet been ready to receive a greater influx of nighttime animation shows. "Let's face it, Bill," he recently remarked. "*The Flintstones* hung in there for six seasons, but do you remember the bum reviews we got on the show for the first two seasons it was on? We were trying to whet the viewers' appetites for an expanded menu of our product and they weren't ready for the main course yet."

Viewers may have been still munching on the appetizers, but we were going to stay in the kitchen working on the entrees. We knew our programs were appealing entertainment, and we were betting that they would want more—during the dinner hour and beyond. *The Jetsons'* saga was not concluded. The series was rerun in syndication on Saturday mornings the following season and were a great success among young viewers. Over the years, despite numerous network shifts, the series continued to build a huge following, and by 1987 we eventually produced fifty-one new episodes of *The Jetsons* that were added to the original shows in syndication.

Although the initial lackluster ratings of *The Jetsons* following its premier were disappointing, we were still proud of the quantum leap the series creatively symbolized at the time. Joe still claims the show was ahead of its time and I'm inclined to agree. Many of the futuristic elements devised for the series were remarkably clever and imaginative. Some of the concepts, in fact, have proved to be downright visionary. In viewing some of the original episodes from that first season, I marvel at how Elroy's television wristwatch and George's household treadmill that seemed so fantastic back in 1962 have become increasingly commonplace items today.

Beyond the gimmickry and gadgetry, however, *The Jetsons* possessed much of the warmth, wit, and humor of our other cartoon shows. The characters were likable, they were funny, and you could tell that they cared about each other. In many ways the human condition never really changes. I think every age will face its dilemmas of apprehension, anticipation, frustration, and confusion, and just enough encouraging success to keep us going. The funhouse reflection of these daily challenges provide the basis for what are basically timeless qualities in family entertainment. Our viewers, I would like to believe, have found these elements consistent in our shows from Stone Age to Space Age, and it is their response that ultimately proved to make *The Jetsons* a perennial favorite show of new generations.

In all frankness, I must confess that hindsight and luck has a lot to do with how I characterize a lot of those old shows today. People kindly term them "classics" now, but in those years any endeavor to "immortalize" these cartoons never entered our minds. By the mid-1960s Joe had built his staff of writers into a solid creative corps capable of developing a profusion of appealing and varied concepts for cartoon pilots.

The majority of those storylines seemed to me at the time wonderfully refreshing in nature. We tackled the production of every new show that sold with as fervent a commitment to cooperative craftsmanship as we had exerted on the last.

Production was a prayerful word to me, for it in essence defined in three syllables my professional motivation and the very reason for my existence in this business. In my mind it actually made no real difference as to what show we were working on in production, for the work itself was always enjoyable regardless of whether it was for Augie Doggie or Baba Looey. A Hanna-Barbera product, was a Hanna-Barbera product and as long as it bore our company name it merited its own measure of professional devotion.

The basic rudiments of limited animation production devised by my partner and me had laid the foundation for our company's industry. Foundations, however, are meant to be built upon, and the dynamics of our increased production compelled continual refinements in production technique and methods.

Over the years, Joe and I have taken our share of heat from critics who have referred to us as purveyors of "cookie cutter" cartoons because of the limited animation system we advanced. Our shows have sometimes been criticized as lacking the artistic appeal of the traditional full animation theatrical shorts, and our characters described as moving in a wooden or mechanical manner.

These are in great part, I believe, analytical observations often made from the standpoint of reviewers enchanted by the sweep in motion picture cartoons. Such pictures, including I might add those of our own Tom and Jerry, were indeed visually wonderful and marvelous examples of what can be achieved in production nourished by lavish budgets.

Joe and I loved these cartoons as much as anyone else. We loved watching them and we loved making them. But I don't believe that spectacle in animation was ever meant to provide the sole element of a cartoon's entertainment appeal. If that had been the case, then animation as an industry might well have entered an indefinite eclipse with the termination of those original motion picture cartoon studios.

Like so many things in life, nature, and culture, the motion picture cartoons and the industry that fostered them once found itself an endangered species faced with the prospect of adapting or dying.

It had been my good luck to watch the animation industry grow up. From 1930 to the mid 1950s, I had seen cartoon entertainment develop from the primitive black-and-white talkie shorts to the rich color productions in Cinemascope. These changes issued from the continual refinement and sophistication of production techniques and methods. The budgets, schedules, and general creative and mechanical scope of cartoonmaking, however, remained constant in the sense that they were all geared to accommodate the production needs of the motion picture medium. The profession radically changed, however, when television entered the picture. Suddenly, the challenge confronting us was not one of the mere continuation of technical advancement, but the grim necessity of surviving as an industry.

What could we do? Well, we could have elected to go out in a blaze of glory with a swan-song, big-screen cartoon that saluted the demise of the animation business. One final Tom and Jerry picture for the road and then maybe a career in real estate. Forget it. That was never a serious option for either Joe Barbera or me.

The very circumstances that compelled us to look to television as a recourse, also provided many of the reasons why it was necessary for animation to embrace a new form. Dispossessed by the silver screen, cartoonmaking either had to conform to the test patterns of the embryonic television medium or disappear altogether.

Anyone who remembers those early, hazy, black-and-white, six-inch images on diminutive screens may smile along with me in recalling how marvelous a phenomenon we thought TV was at the time. Never mind the reduction in size, scope, and spectacle from big-screen movies. This was an intimate medium with a potential for colossal growth that by 1957 had already become dramatically apparent by the flourishing variety of programs.

The scale of production involved in turning out such a consistent flow of weekly entertainment imposed revolutionary challenges for those of us in Hollywood who were essentially direct transplants from the motion picture industry. A myriad of creative, mechanical, and technical adjustments confronted us if we wanted to carve out our niche in TV. They all essentially funneled down to two distinct concerns: time and money. Gone forever were the deep pockets and lenient deadlines that allocated dollars and indulgent production schedules to us with such golden profusion. In their place appeared initial shoestring budgets of daunting severity and that implacable television specter known as the air date.

Like radio, television from its virtual inception adopted as a trademark concept the series format as a means of cultivating an intimacy with its audience. Weekly one-hour and half-hour programs were the staple fare for a viewing market that consumed on a nightly basis an infinitely greater volume of entertainment than the public's occasional visits to the movies ever did.

The differing complexions of the two markets were vividly evident. Television had become a daily and nightly viewing habit, while motion picture attendance became relegated to a periodic family "event." Personally speaking, going to the movies had always been an enjoyable occasion for my wife and kids and me. But the accessibility of television as a kind of personal theatre with free admission significantly diluted the mystique of film entertainment when adventure, romance, the news, and laughs could be had as items all included in the price of our monthly electric bill.

It was at times a little unnerving for some of us who had allied ourselves with television production in those early days—to see in our own homes the undeniable magnetic influence that that glass-and-metal box commanded over our families and household. It was spellbinding. Hour after hour after hour of constant broadcast entertainment were absorbed by mesmerized viewers including ourselves and our own families. Television viewing was definitely a personal matter and our kids, neighbors, and friends were the very representatives of the ravenous market that demanded from us an unceasing flow of intimate and immediate entertainment that would a few minutes later become yesterday's reruns.

This was a form of enchantment entirely different than the ritualistic occasional reward of "going out" and splurging on tickets that purchased the velvet seats of a film palace every weekend. America was beginning to stay at home more and more, and to reaffirm—over Jiffy Pop and Dr. Pepper—viewer loyalties that were growing from repeated exposure to television series stars and their ongoing adventures.

Television air dates provided the axis upon which the entire industry relentlessly turned. These were broadcast deadlines that ruled producers with an iron hand. Production schedules were high-stakes regimens upon whose efficiency or inaptitude we would either prosper or perish.

As cartoon producers, we generally had thirteen weeks to deliver thirteen half-hour shows for a cartoon series at a rate of one show a week. This actual production schedule was preceded by an intense period of promotional and development activity. A proposal for a new show, consisting of a sample script and prototype artwork displaying characters and settings, was initially presented to network or agency executives. This was the "pitch," and its presentation was entirely in Joe's province. In short order, my partner had developed into a formidable salesman for our company with a proficiency in closing these deals that often astonished and occasionally in later years dismayed me.

In those early years we were, of course, grateful for every minute of airtime secured. But as the popularity of our shows increased, the momentum of supply and demand shifted dramatically, and I eventually found our units surfeited with production work resulting from a growing volume of sales.

If the show sold, we would receive an order from either the network or series sponsor to deliver the standard quota of thirteen half-hour shows to be delivered on time for the debut of the fall season. The months between January and September, when the first show aired, were committed to a season of relentless production activity in which we were required to deliver a show at a rate of one a week. The entire production process was geared to meet this weekly deadline. We were required to deliver what was known as an answer print, in essence the entire show on film that included all the music, dialogue, and effects synchronized to the picture. The answer print became the master print from which copies were made.

The creative demands of such an endeavor were intense. All of the elements—from conceptualizing the story, developing models for any new or additional characters in the show, refining the artwork, and casting and directing the voice talent to the final dubbing session—had to be completed within that thirteen-week period.

Such stringent production demands would have been virtually impossible to meet if we had been making these cartoons in full animation. The stern curtailment of time and money was the unrelenting onus of television. The limited animation techniques we'd devised, I believe, were entirely in scale with the visual dimensions and production boundaries of television. In addition to achieving the necessary adaptation to the small screen with this method, Joe and I were both convinced that this style of animation had distinct and vivid entertainment merits of its own.

By the strategic filming and artful timing of selected images, this new animation conveyed a convincing illusion of action that was enhanced by clever and descriptive dialogue. The characters may have moved in a limited form, but they walked, ran, flew, and most critically, talked, joked, or sang in a way that made them appear alive and real to our viewers.

A lot of the criticism that belittled TV cartoons, I feel, issued from the same attitudes that rebuked television itself. Animation production for the small screen pretty much grew up with television. Like the development of any art form or industry, television had to undergo its primitive age along with the horseless carriage, the telephone, and even motion pictures themselves.

Every one of them in their time faced their share of derision and were dismissed as mere novelties impertinently attempting to supplant the revered traditional forms that preceded them. Such lessons of history might be better employed if critics, reviewers, and analysts were encouraged more frequently to employ hindsight of past progress as a means of embracing a more appreciative vision of those things that augur the future.

Joe and I believed in television. We were both moved by the exciting commercial and creative potential it implied in those early years. If we had not envisioned, for example, the eventuality of color television, we would never have ventured to produce our first cartoons with full color artwork while the shows were still being broadcast in black and white.

In all frankness, we felt that we had no choice *but* to believe in its destiny if we were to have any professional future in the business we loved. Changing times had brought us a commercial break, and some compelling challenges in having a hand both in building a business and developing an aspect of a new medium.

Despite our optimism, however, neither of us ever imagined the amazing technological and artistic advancements that ultimately transformed television entertainment into such a nonpareil art of its own. What we were lucky enough to maintain a hands-on relationship with, however, was the dynamic refinement and growth of our own cartoon industry. Limited animation production has come a long way from the first vintage Ruff and Reddy and Huckleberry Hound cartoons. Over the years the pictures have grown more fully dimensional and the special effects increasingly stunning, and the foundation crafts of writing, animating, and editing have acquired a high gloss of stunning excellence.

It is said that what *evolves* must first be *involved*. Neither Joe Barbera nor I really felt that there would ever be any lasting limits to limited animation. But once upon a time, we could see that if cartoons were to survive to grow up, they would first need a new beginning.

Chapter Thirteen

Old Guards and New Breeds

C artoons can create their own animated version of Never-Never Land. Unlike the fabled realm of Peter Pan and Captain Hook, however, the natural laws of growth in life are not necessarily nullified, although they are often suspended. In cartoons, children sometimes do grow up—especially when their maturing and growth can provide a bright appeal to new generations of the animation audience.

By the 1970s, many of our original viewers who first joined us as youngsters to watch the premier episodes of *Ruff and Reddy*, *Huckleberry Hound*, and *Yogi Bear* were young adults with kids of their own. Time was marching on in the cartoon business, and considering that the tempo of this passage for our characters on film was at a rate of ninety feet a minute and twenty-four frames a second, Huck and Yogi hadn't appeared to have aged a whisker. Ink and paint and celluloid can work wonders in preserving the youthful images of these celebrities. Joe and I knew, however, that if we wanted to keep the magic alive in our programming, we'd have to forge ahead and produce an increasing volume of fresh story material, contemporary characters, and expanded program formats that would continue to captivate a current audience.

During the first two decades following the formation of our studio, television had made remarkable advancements in the development of its programming. The live-action shows, both comic and dramatic, presented to audiences during the 1960s and 1970s mirrored both the lingering innocence and growing sophistication of that era. Color TV was still regarded by millions of viewers as an engrossing phenomenon. The small screen, in short, had done us proud in justifying our faith in its potential, and Joe and I were hoping that our contribution to the medium would be just as praiseworthy.

As the antennae of its age, television reflected the mood of the times. Although westerns were still going strong during the 1960s and 1970s, new breeds of program concepts designed to appeal to a new generation of adolescent and teenage viewers began to appear in force. Pop music shows like *Sonny and Cher* and *The Monkees* featuring long-haired youngsters sporting bell-bottom jeans and electric guitars showcased the current trends of American youth. Although this shaggy, mod look definitely raised the eyebrows of many critics, I generally found these shows to be pretty wholesome and spirited fare. It was lively, clean entertainment and if they could become hits as live-action shows, they could be just as much fun to watch as cartoons.

By now I had several grandchildren who had joined the ranks of a new guard of Saturday morning cartoon viewership, and they handily helped keep me current on "What's hot and what's not." Despite the increasing cultural crossover that develops with each new generation, the traditional adage that "Boys will be boys, and girls will be girls" still seemed to apply just as aptly to my grandchildren as they did with my kids when they were young'uns.

David's two boys, Bill and John, and Bonnie's sons, David and Philip, were still typical products of the old masculine recipe of equal parts "slugs and snails and puppydog tails." Following the natural inclinations of rambunctious adolescents, they were definitely more prone to favor the action superhero adventures of such macho mavericks as *The Six-Million Dollar Man* or the mystic martial artist Caine in *Kung Fu*.

David's two girls, Laurie and Molly, and their cousin Emily definitely preferred the domestic family shows like *The Brady Bunch* and *Family Affair*. Aside from an early tomboy phase in their adolescence, my granddaughters all emerged as decidedly feminine and somewhat traditionally romantic in temperament, although the girls also displayed a liberated side to their personalities in their admiration of *Wonder Woman* and *The Bionic Woman*.

With seven grandchildren, I had an ample adolescent support

group to help me bridge any generation gap regarding TV viewing trends. Basically, kids will always be kids. Youngsters today seem to enjoy many of the same fundamentals of entertainment that I did as a child or my kids did when they were children. The elements of action, adventure, color, and humor regardless of the presentation are in my estimation qualities of good, wholesome entertainment that will always hold everlasting appeal for the perennial child. Still, given all of this, every generation cherishes its own idea of what is fun and entertaining according to the unique season of their childhood.

It's always gratifying of course, when the basic premise of a cartoon show proves durable enough to appeal to succeeding generations of viewers. Happily, we had gleaned a lot of entertaining mileage out of *The Flintstones*. The show went into syndication in 1972. For my own grandkids, watching *The Flintstones* was an automatic given. By the time my granddaughter Laurie was eight, she had developed a personal relationship to the show that she unabashedly felt put her on a first-name basis with the cast lead. "Grandpa," she would often declare in blithe disregard of any formal reference to *The Flintstones* as a series. "Grandpa, I wanna see Fred tonight!"

Despite such heartening evidence of the big guy's perennial charisma, Joe and I were nevertheless determined that Fred and Wilma as "popular primitives" did not descend into becoming cultural dinosaurs. In our efforts to insure that our Neolithic Notables retained a fresh appeal to young viewers, we decided to expand the format to bring a second generation of characters more into the spotlight. In the original *Flintstones* series, Fred and Wilma's daughter Pebbles and Barney and Betty's son Bamm Bamm had been introduced as infants and seemed to have immediately won the viewers' hearts.

We reasoned that a new series based upon the adventures of these Jurassic juveniles as teenagers would be an engaging way to remain current with the adolescent audiences. *Pebbles and Bamm Bamm* premiered in 1971 and re-introduced the kids as students of Bedrock High School who tooled around in their own set of prehistoric wheels together with a clean-cut company of other cave-kids. Appropriate to a television era that popularized programs featuring such pop music groups as *The Partridge Family*, Pebbles and Bamm Bamm obligingly entertained viewers with lively performances with their own prehistoric "rock" band.

Spunky and precocious kids' groups, of course, have been a staple of classic comedy since the old Little Rascals and Our Gang shorts produced by Hal Roach. Following this ever-reliable format, two talented writers named Ken Spears and Joe Ruby in the late 1960s came up with a set of characters and accompanying story premise for a cartoon show that was to become one of our most popular and successful series for Saturday morning television.

Scooby-Doo, Where Are You? premiered in September 1969 and introduced as its title character a timid but lovable Great Dane with a voracious appetite that vividly imparted new meaning to the term "chow hound." Scooby's master was a likable but disheveled youth aptly named Shaggy, who shared both his canine's craven instincts and insatiable craving for food.

The basic plotlines of the *Scooby-Doo* series generally placed the main characters in supernatural adventures involving ominous haunted houses, ghosts and other mysterious menaces, which all served to emphasize for laughs our unlikely heroes' instinct to "advance to the rear."

Playing the "flight with fright rather than fight" theme to the hilt, Scooby and Shaggy became two of the most engaging if unlikely heroes of any of the cartoon series we turned out during that era. As I recall from enlightening chats with my grandkids, the period during the late 1960s and early 1970s was predominantly characterized by a kind of cultural revolution exhorting our youth to "do their own thing." One of the biggest reasons for Scooby-Doo's great appeal, I think, was that the show in certain ways captured the sound as well as the look of the period in all of its flower power.

This feeling for the time was enhanced by the great voice characterization of Shaggy by Casey Kasem, who even in 1969 had achieved considerable popularity as a prominent radio personality. Casey recalled in a letter to me recently how his input on one occasion directly influenced a major alteration in Shaggy's nutritional lifestyle. The story is related with Casey's inimitable congenial humor and charm and is quoted here as Casey wrote it:

"Hanna-Barbera is a place where you feel valuable and respected as an actor. There's always a lot of good food, nutritious snacks, fruit, etc. available when you come in to work. The staff is open to suggestions too, like the time I turned vegetarian—and wondered if my *Scooby-Doo* character, Shaggy, couldn't become a vegetarian, also. 'No problem,' Gordon replied. And for the last ten years of the show, Shaggy and Scooby-Doo *both* were vegetarians!"

True to the spirit of the lyrics Bob Dylan's song, "The times, they were a changin'." This transformation had a vivid impact on altering and expanding the nature of television animation programs both in story premises and production qualities.

Following the lead of live action trends, Joe and I concluded that generating the *fun* in television entertainment no longer just meant presenting *funny* shows. Science fiction tales, superheroes, and secret agents were all making inroads into the primetime and general television market. Crimefighters like Batman and The Green Hornet were reincarnated from the comic books and Old Republic serials into new video versions, replete with updated vehicles and costumes and endowed with contemporary attitudes and dialogue scripted to appeal to the tastes of a new generation of young viewers.

Our primary, and I think, most significant foray into this genre of action-adventure entertainment was the creation of *The Adventures of Jonny Quest*, which premiered as a primetime series in the fall of 1964 on ABC. The debut of *Jonny Quest* marked a sharp departure in style from Hanna-Barbera's traditional stable of shows featuring cute and funny characters who seldom contended with anything more menacing than an irate park ranger or a stuffy and belligerent boss ranting at the show's harried hero.

Jonny Quest by dramatic contrast was wide-open action and suspense. It was pure escape fare that literally erupted on the TV screen in a fast-paced sequence featuring exciting images of stalking mummies, slithering serpents, high-speed chases, and climactic explosions in a zestfully rousing weekly opener for each show.

Appropriate to its futuristic themes, *Jonny Quest* also marked a quantum leap ahead in production methods as well. Producing an action-animated series in those days was an ambitious undertaking primarily because, as the term implied, it demanded so much action.

Unlike any of our comedic characters who could generally carry the show based upon the charm of their cuteness, wit, and humor and with minimal suggestive movement, action heroes and villains had to be lively, animated swashbucklers. In addition, their heroics—true to the tradition of comic strip vividness—needed a fast-moving sequence of thrilling cliff-hanger action in order to project the greatest possible impact upon our viewers.

Such vitality and pacing, translated into the logistics of production, quite frankly meant more money for more drawings per foot of film. By current standards, *Jonny Quest* was an expensive series to make, but thanks in great part to Joe Barbera's compelling sales presentation to the network—which featured an action-packed sample reel of explosive thrills with promise of more to come—we had the budget for it.

The payoff was that *Jonny Quest* became one of our most popular shows, and it eventually launched a whole platoon of other Hanna-Barbera cartoon series in the action-adventure genre, including among others *The Fantastic Four*, *Space Ghost*, *The Herculoids*, and *The Galaxy Trio*.

While we pushed ourselves to keep up with the kids through new kinds of TV shows—it was stern necessity after all that compelled Joe and me to begin our careers in television animation through the vehicle of limited animation—neither of us ever lost our love of the full animation film as a high art form. In the MGM years, the studio found theatrical shorts expensive enough. MGM, along with Warner Bros. and other animation units, left the full-length animated films to Disney. In those early Hanna-Barbera years, we produced two animated films, *Hey There, It's Yogi Bear* and *A Man Called Flintstone*. Over the years, production methods nourished by increasingly larger budgets had allowed us to become more sophisticated as well as ambitious in our creative endeavors.

The crown of our mutual artistic aspirations as partners was achieved in 1973 when Hanna-Barbera, in association with Paramount, released a lovingly crafted, fully animated feature film called *Charlotte's Web*. Based upon E.B. White's beloved children's book, the film, I feel, exquisitely captured the spirit of his poignant tale of friendship and humility. All the elements came together beautifully—Debbie Reynolds was a wonderful Charlotte and Paul Lynde brought the right sparks to Templeton.

Charlotte's Web had a warm reception—critically and popularly. We were especially honored when the animation industry gave it an Annie Award. This film remains one of my personal favorites as a showcase of the best of what our people were creating, an endeavor of stunning excellence.

While programming facelifts, revisions, and futuristic concepts mirrored changing times in our industry, Joe and I were also experiencing yet another shift in our own professional evolution. In 1967, my partner and I were approached by representatives from the Taft Broadcasting Company with an offer to purchase our studio. By that time, Hanna-Barbera Productions had been in operation for a decade. During those first ten years we'd been able to consistently net some impressive numbers as a profitable enterprise and ongoing concern in what was then still regarded as a relatively new industry.

The volume of our sales and the amplifying profit margin grossed in our production had attracted the attention of several agencies interested in investing in the company, including Screen Gems, Universal Studios, and Taft Broadcasting. Each of these companies made substantial offers, but Joe and I ultimately decided to accept the Taft proposal; we felt it to be generous from both the financial standpoint and the overall spirit of its creative attitude towards the business of making cartoons.

Contrary to some mischievous public speculation at the time, our decision to sell the studio was not due to any personal conflict between Joe and me, nor any growing professional estrangement. The truth of the matter was that both of us felt that the transaction signified a gratifying plateau of success in our professional lives.

Hanna-Barbera had prospered and her prospects for growth seemed brighter than ever. When Joe and I first formed the company, we were both willing to "do without" for as long as it took, providing we could continue doing what we loved best—making cartoons. During the first months of operation, we had paid ourselves a salary of fifty dollars a week in addition to the aid of a company credit card which we used to buy our lunches. Our stock had risen impressively since those days and we were exceedingly proud of the efficient and gainful distinction the company had earned over the years.

The offer from Taft Broadcasting to purchase Hanna-Barbera Productions was actually a tremendous validation to us. The Taft people impressed both Joe and me as being direct, candid, and professionally respectful of the artistic nature of our business. What they wished to acquire, we were frankly advised, was a sound bullish enterprise that was both financially dynamic and creatively vital in both its current operation and future projections. The Taft executives were not kidding themselves. They were investors, not producers, and they felt they needed a professional alliance with the two guys named Bill Hanna and Joe Barbera if that investment was to continue to thrive.

Given that understanding, my partner and I signed a contract with Taft stipulating that Joe and I would continue to run the studio and maintain complete control of its operations. It was an amicable deal, particularly since the transfer of ownership to our new parent company also released us from a multitude of complex concerns involving taxes, insurance, and other maintenance responsibilities attendant to ownership.

In addition, the figure negotiated for the studio's sale to Taft would compensate Joe and me with more money than either of us had ever dreamed of earning in our lives. It was a gratifying, in fact awesome, financial validation for two little boys from the Depression to whom wealth for the most part meant paid mortgages, a decent bank account, and working at a job that we felt we could do better than most anyone else.

Well, we had the money and we still had the job. We hadn't exactly gone from rags to riches but our professional origins had certainly been modest, if not entirely obscure. Together, the kid from Brooklyn and the Boy Scout from Watts had put in a good run, and we were still picking up the pace.

The transition of ownership to Taft was effected so smoothly that most of our employees scarcely noticed the shift. Studio policy remained the same, except for the fact that Joe and I could indulge in a few sighs of relief regarding our relinquishment of some of the more tedious administrative paperwork.

Looking back at that first relatively rippleless switch to Taft, I couldn't help feeling somewhat pensive and more than a little restive. It was something like taking a breather gazing out at the vista below from halfway up the mountain you've climbed. The past looked wonderful in retrospect, but our future looked even better. Hanna-Barbera Studio still seemed like a very good place to be, but only if we kept moving.

Chapter Fourteen

Joint Ventures

My business partner has always had a distinctly joyous gift for enjoying the good life. This aptitude, which includes a love of gourmet cuisine and a healthy circulation of what Joe humorously refers to as his "good Sicilian blood," are factors which I believe have significantly contributed to his perennial youthfulness and generally excellent health. I've managed to hold together fairly well myself over the years, although for entirely different reasons, owing primarily perhaps to a stubborn Irish ancestry and a diet of home-cooked meals of hash, stews, or beans, which were often the products of my own stove-top efforts.

Away from the studio, Joe and I led entirely different lives and were probably a classic example of how opposites attract without *subtracting* from our respective individual natures. This was a congeniality that has worked well for us over the years—despite persistent and erroneous gossip insisting that Bill Hanna and Joe Barbera could not stand the sight of each other, and that we continued to maintain our partnership only as an impersonal business operation.

During our long and eventful professional association, Joe and I have had our share of disagreements and occasionally, some real settos. What effective partnership has not? I remember how one business consultant ventured the observation that if you never argued with your partner, you didn't need a partner. Differing perspectives, opinions, and viewpoints, including those adamantly held, provide some of the most critically positive attributes of a creative association. But that, in essence, is the reason why there are two names on our company logo, and one of the primary causes of what has proven to be our longlasting creative viability.

The actual reasons for our differing lifestyles quite simply is that Joe and I are two different people. We've joked on more than one occasion about how the often stark contrasts of our respective ideas of having a good time might make prime material for a situation comedy that could give *The Odd Couple* a run for its money. Over the years, we've both purchased various properties, and our choices of real-estate investments reflect as vividly as anything else our different personalities.

Joe loves the sunshine and the warm weather. He owns a piece of land in Palm Springs occupied by an opulent abode, a tennis court, and a small orchard that raises some of the largest and most luscious grapefruit and lemons I've ever tasted. Hand him his sunglasses, provide a lounge and reservations at one of the top restaurants in the area, and Joe has attained nirvana.

My creature comforts, so to speak, have tended to be earthier. More like "critter" comforts. Since my early days as a Boy Scout, I've enjoyed heading off for the "tall and uncut," camping out and cooking out. Several years ago, I purchased 150 acres of a large ranch in Northern California which is situated in Fall River Valley between Mount Lassen and Mount Shasta. The ranch is located on the edge of a pine forest and consists of a two-story ranch house of ten thousand square feet. Near the house there are several large natural springs of beautiful clear bubbling water.

These springs flow through the mountains toward the Pacific Ocean to form a confluence known as Eastman Lake, which then feeds into the Fall River. The country there abounds with wildlife, including an ever-flourishing population of quail that enchanted Vi so much that she promptly christened our spread "Quail Ranch" and the ranch house the "Quail House."

I had first learned about the region while still a young'un working at Harman-Ising Studio. A neighbor of mine named Jim Christie had told me about the great fishing in that part of the country. One year during my vacation, I had gone up to see for myself and fallen in love with the place. It was literally a sportsman's Canaan, and the water from those pristine springs was the purest and sweetest I had ever tasted.

Fall River Valley had staked a claim on my heart, and although

I admittedly yearned to own a home amid such beauty, I never dared hope, back in 1930, that such a dream would ever come true. Still, it's funny how certain things can take hold of you. Summer after summer, I had been drawn back to Fall River Valley, and the place became a kind of Promised Land in my mind.

If I recall my Bible stories correctly, it took the Children of Israel forty years to reach their destination of a land flowing with milk and honey. It seems no less miraculous to me today that after fifty years of enchantment with the place, in 1980 I acquired my own Promised Land abundant with glowing rainbow trout and dusky, sure-footed, wild mule deer.

The land was virtually undeveloped when we obtained title, and Violet and I spent many a happy day pacing off footage and discussing how we wanted the ranch house to be built. Vi was as excited as I was with the ranch and as exuberant as a schoolgirl. She virtually bubbled with ideas for certain special features to be built into the house, including a nice big kitchen, and windows for all of the bedrooms. One of the most interesting attractions Vi envisioned was the inclusion of a mud room, which would allow occupants coming in from inclement weather to comfortably shed wet or muddy clothing before entering the main house. This was a feature that had been introduced to Violet during the years she had visited our son's family in Connecticut to babysit our first grandchildren. Always a meticulous hostess, Violet had been impressed by the facility, and it was promptly included in the initial plans that I drew up for construction of the ranch house.

Although we engaged a contractor for the actual construction of the place, I enjoyed flying up there on weekends when time allowed to keep my hand in on some little carpentry or painting project. This was a legacy from my dad. I have always loved engaging in manual labor and the special kind of healthy, unpretentious, hands-on fellowship that it seems to foster. There is a certain timeless integrity that comes with flesh and blood and bone and muscle working with wood or stone, iron tools, or, in fact, any of the earthy elements. The salt of the earth is a miracle mineral that can be found in the sweat of our own brows and in the absorption of any good work. I generally found perspiring to be inspiring.

Still, I have found that there is a considerable difference between the internal stress often connected to white collar demands as opposed to the external exertions of blue collar ones. While I made the choice early on to follow a profession outside of the field of manual labor, I believe that the recreational and creative release of such activity has done a lot to keep me grounded in my life.

Construction of the ranch house was completed in about a year, but one of the ongoing joys of the property for me was that I always managed to contrive some other improvement of the place that could keep me busy at the sawhorses during visits. One of the principal reasons Vi and I decided to build Quail House on the expansive scale that we did was to provide ample and comfortable accommodations for our growing circle of family and friends. This had been an incentive in our lives regarding anything we chose to acquire from the first.

My wife today has pretty much remained the same girl I first met back in 1935. Throughout all the failures and fortunes of our lives, she has remained remarkably unaffected by the designs of high society, opulent trends in affluent lifestyles, or the political intrigues of the entertainment business.

Neither Violet nor I have ever been inclined toward an active membership in the so-called jet set. I imagine that such statements, from people perceived by the public as being affluent, are generally met with skepticism. Nowadays it admittedly seems to be a trend for folks in a higher income tax bracket to issue disclaimers regarding the opulence of their lifestyles. "Shucks, folks—I put on my pants one leg at a time just like you do" or "How many beds can you sleep in or meals can you eat?" Inveigling questions, but they could ring hollow I'll admit, to anyone with only a couple pairs of jeans, sleeping in a Murphy bed, and living on Spam.

I was not a stranger to any of those experiences during the Depression, but I never believed that they would be permanent in my own life. Hard times had taught us early on to live one day at a time because the immediate necessity of survival didn't really allow you to do much more. I happened to be lucky. I landed a job that also provided me with a profession I loved. That to me was prosperity. I was earning while I was learning, and one of my primary realizations during this process was that there was a wealth in my work. Affluence to most people, I think, means having enough money to do what they want to do whether it's playing polo, going on a cruise, or reveling in a nonstop nightlife. There is, admittedly, a glamour to all of those things, but none of it ever appealed to my wife or me.

The myth of money is that it can buy a kind of fairy-tale happiness based upon what you have rather than who you are or what you do. Now don't get me wrong. I don't denigrate money. It is an invaluable resource that has enabled me to joyfully function according to what seemed right for my own nature. Our beautiful ranch house and pastoral acreage was in fact a youthful fantasy come true, and money had a lot to do with bringing about its fulfillment.

Happiness for Violet has always meant a loving involvement with family and friends. Fulfillment for me has come through absorption in my work and the fellowship of my coworkers and loved ones. The ranch provided a serene, restorative environment that invited us both to return to the innocent daydreaming that we had done as kids, when the Quail House seemed little more than an intangible dream itself. Somehow, through yearning and earning, it had emerged as an astonishing dividend—the result of getting paid for a job that I had always loved for the sheer fun of it. In a way I think I have had the best of both worlds. I have always been paid to enjoy what I have done for a living, while some other folks have had to toil at a job they consider to be drudgery in order to be able to pay for their off-work enjoyment.

"Status" admittedly is a word that is often used to characterize the affluent in society. Vi and I have been exceedingly fortunate in our lives but frankly, the term "status" remains a somewhat alien word to both of us, for it really wasn't included in the glossary of values we learned from our families or during the Depression.

Neither did the acquisition of "status" gain any greater significance to us as a desirable goal while we worked to raise our family, pay off the mortgage, or put the kids through college. In all candor, we very well knew the definition of the word, but its actual meaning seemed irrelevant when compared with other "s-words" such as solvency, security, and sharing.

All of these priorities issue from instinctive human ambition. It is an inborn trait to want to better yourself, and that is a drive I feel should be expressed rather than suppressed. Among the inherent principles of self-respect I was raised with was a distinct conviction to make the most of your opportunities and resources.

Desire, ideas, money, and even necessity are, as far as I'm concerned, assets to be utilized. They are all grist for the mill. The appreciation of these assets, when creatively and conscientiously applied through the experiences of work, is a vivid part of the business of living. In all candor, money was never significant to me as an end in itself, but rather as a means to an end. It was a resource in pro-

Ruff and Reddy, the first creations of Hanna-Barbera Productions. *(© Hanna-Barbera Productions Inc.)*

The Huckleberry Hound gang in 1959. In the rear, writer Charles Shows and Joe Barbera. In front, Don Messick, Daws Butler, me, and artist George Gordon.

Yogi and Boo Boo

This award we got to keep for a change: Hanna-Barbera's first Emmy for *The Huckleberry Hound Show* in 1960. Joining Joe and me is producer Alex Lovy.

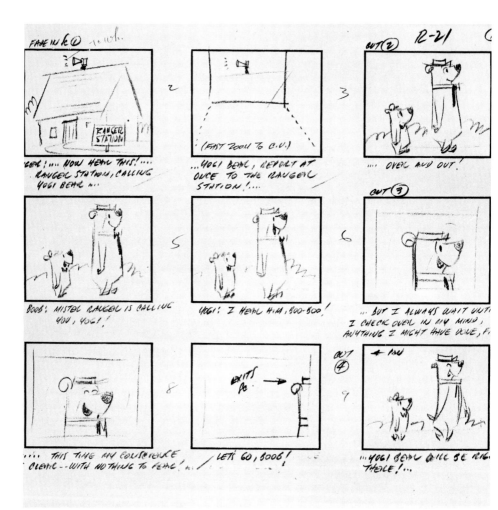

A first-season storyboard for Yogi Bear.

Early model sheet for Fred Flintstone. Note that "Gladstone"—a name nobody was happy with—has been crossed out for the new, improved name.

(© Hanna-Barbera Productions Inc.)

The Flintstones—America's first primetime animated TV family. *(© Hanna-Barbera Productions Inc.)*

Home Sweet Home—
the new Hanna-Barbera
studios in 1963.

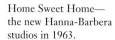

Meet the Flintstones: Voiceover artists Alan Reed (*Fred*), Jean VanderPyl (*Wilma*), Bea Benaderet (*Betty Rubble*), and Mel Blanc (*Barney Rubble* and *Dino*). (© *Hanna-Barbera Productions Inc.*)

Huckleberry Hound

Secret Squirrel

Dynomutt

Quick Draw McGraw and Baba Looey

Magilla Gorilla

The Jetsons

Scooby-Doo

Augie Doggie and Doggie Daddy

Tom and Jerry

Atom Ant

The Adventures of Jonny Quest ushered in a new era of action-oriented cartoons.
(© *Hanna-Barbera Productions Inc.*)

Building the *Galatea* in Santa Barbera, 1966.

A cast of friends aboard the *Galatea*: animators Jay Sarbry, Carl Urbano, Lefty Callahan, Irv Spence, me, and musician Norm Langerak.

Charlotte's Web—a glorious return to full animation.

Heidi's Song (1982) proved a disappointment at the box office, but it was a beloved Hanna-Barbera theatrical production with lush artwork.

Hanna-Barbera make the Hollywood Walk of Fame in 1976 (with Jane Withers). *(Kelly Associates)*

Hoyt Curtin has composed many memorable cartoon themes for Hanna-Barbera.

In 1986, I visited Manila in the Philippines to oversee Hanna-Barbera-contracted animation from Optifex International. I'm briefing the Background Department Supervisor while Jo Harn (*far left*), Production Manager, and Jerry Smith (*left*), our Overseas Consultant, look on. Jerry Smith became general manager of Hanna-Barbera's Philippines operation in 1987.

Receiving the Governors Award at the 1988 Emmys ceremony.

Joe and I meet Steven Spielberg at Universal in 1988.

Top Cat and the Beverly Hills Cats. *(© Hanna-Barbera Productions Inc.)*

Friz Freleng and I enjoyed a long friendship after working briefly together on the ill-fated Captain and the Kids at MGM. Decades later, he joined us at Hanna-Barbera. Here, we're at the 1993 Annie Awards.

(© Hanna-Barbera Productions Inc.)

Joe and I were inducted into the Television Academy Hall of Fame in 1994, with, among others, Oprah Winfrey.

John Goodman (Fred Flintstone) and I toast the film version of *The Flintstones*, 1994.

Vi and me today.

Still at it: creating the cartoon short *Hard Luck Duck* for Turner Broadcasting and the Cartoon Network (1994).

Scooby-Doo, Shaggy, Scrappy, and the Boo Brothers.
(© *Hanna-Barbera Productions Inc.*)

I even assisted with the recording of the orchestra for *Hard Luck Duck*.

Joe and I celebrating the fiftieth anniversary of our creative partnership.

duction that expedited the expression of professional talent, industrialism, and efficiency. Money helped me get the job done in areas of endeavor in which I always strove to excel both artistically and in the way of business. It was often a critical balancing act and I sometimes fell short of my goals, but I never ceased to value the challenge or the means to meet it.

Money along with a decent reputation can provide you with that indispensable professional leverage known as clout. Again, this is an asset that is meant to be creatively utilized rather than exploited, and anything done out of sheer vanity as far as I'm concerned is a form of exploitation.

There have been occasions when I have not hesitated a moment to exert a degree of so-called clout when I felt that a little extra muscle was needed to meet an air date or insure fulfillment of some critical professional or business obligation. Again, money can be power, but like any potent force it demands respect and carries responsibility.

But meanwhile, back at the ranch . . . Violet and I were able to indulge in some real Western-style hospitality for family, friends, and on occasion, business associates from various ad agencies that sponsored our shows. Everyone loved the ranch. It was impossible not to fall under the pastoral spell of the place.

The Quail House features a back porch of about 125 feet that spans the length of the west side of the house. At suppertime, we'd hold barbecues on the porch and sit with our guests watching the sunset on the clear-water springs as the fading light gradually seemed to gild the water's surface with a lovely golden hue.

At twilight, the dusk shadows eventually merge into the evening darkness. An occasional mule deer or two might venture across the clearing and disappear into the woods. I've read where various cultures revere the sunset as a sacred ceremony. At Quail House, we've shared countless sunsets with family and friends and sat in quiet admiration and celebration as alpenglow turned into starlight.

Away from the ranch and closer to home, I also owned and enjoyed for several years a number of boats upon whose decks I spent some of the happiest leisure hours of my life. This was, again, a passion from my early youth.

Most children, I think, have an instinctive fascination for water early on. In my own case, that fascination included the adventure of sailing. Whenever I was around water, I wanted to have a boat in it.

I built my first boat when I was about ten or twelve years old and running errands for my dad's construction crew. Taking advantage of the available scrap lumber, nails, and other materials, I set about building a little kayak about eight feet in length which I patterned on a similar craft I had enviously seen another kid a few years older than myself sailing.

I don't recall many details about the actual construction other than the fact that I covered the hull with canvas and painted it in an effort to waterproof the craft. When it was done, my kayak was hardly a thing of beauty, and not nearly as impressive looking as the forerunner model that inspired it. None of that mattered to me, however, compared to the pure elation I felt when I launched the little vessel into the beckoning sewage waters of Bologna Creek and found it seaworthy!

So many years later, while still working at MGM, I spent several weekends with my brother-in-law Leonard Gamble, customizing the interior of a twenty-six-foot cabin cruiser I ordered built by the Lindwall Boat Works in Santa Barbara.

The boat was towed on a trailer to my home in North Hollywood and maneuvered into the backyard. The hull was so large that we had to cut off a corner of the house's roof to get the craft in. There it remained for about a year while Leonard and I installed the craft's refrigerator, galley, and head, along with two bunks. As a final touch we lavished several coats of varnish and paint on the craft.

The project took us many weekends throughout that year to complete in our backyard, but when it was done, it was a thing of beauty and sported a trim hull powered by a sixty-horsepower marine diesel engine.

On the day of the boat's launching, the boat was towed back up to Santa Barbara. Along the way Leonard and I stopped at a liquor store and bought the cheapest bottle of champagne we could find for the boat's christening. Taking care not to chip the vessel's paint job, we broke the bottle over the bow and named the boat the *Bonnie Dee* after my two kids. That was a profound moment. I had become the captain of my first vessel, and standing beside me was my best friend, who, upon raising anchor, had also become my first mate on many a voyage to come.

Leonard Gamble was about the nearest thing to a brother I have ever had in my life. We had been boyhood chums, and as young bachelors dated the twin sisters who eventually became our wives. Unlike most of my other associates, Leonard was one of very few close friends who never became involved in the animation business.

Following graduation from high school, Leonard had gone on to pursue a business degree at Stanford University while I worked on my apprenticeship at Harman-Ising Studio. But the diversity of our professional paths and the respective traits appropriate to a career in accounting as opposed to one in making cartoons were differences that never affected our friendship.

Leonard was the soul of practicality, reserved and conscientious and diligent in all of the details of any project or activity he undertook. His unfailing reliability and steadfastness provided effective counterpoints to my own admittedly more spontaneous and aggressive nature. There were times, I'd like to believe, when my venturesome impulses were a source of joyful stimulation to Leonard's generally reticent nature. I certainly found Leonard's unassuming efficiency to often be of great reassurance when we embarked on many of our sailing adventures together. Ours was a crewmanship surpassingly free of mutiny. Leonard was the navigator and I was the pilot. While I tended the engines, it was Leonard who helped keep us on course by keeping track of the maps, charts, and weather reports on our voyages. In short, we balanced each other out as friends and mates who alternately sustained or encouraged each other.

Boats have a way of growing on you. This was literally true in my own life and eventually led to me selling the *Bonnie Dee* to help finance the building of a sleek, custom fifty-three-foot yacht that became my pride and joy for many years. It took over a year and a half to complete construction of the craft, which I once again contracted to the Lindwall Boatworks.

Leonard and I drove up to Santa Barbara where the craft was being built practically every weekend during those months. We volunteered our services sanding the decks and industriously applying several primary coats of paint to the hull. To this extent we were allowed to contribute our efforts by the boatmaker, Paul Lindwall, although he sternly forbade us to venture beyond brushing on the undercoats. We were allowed, as far as the boat's cosmetics were concerned, to work on anything that didn't show. A meticulous craftsman, Paul planned to apply the finishing coats, trim, and detail work himself.

The new boat blossomed like a rare orchid. She sat up on a lofty wooden framework of construction scaffolding as the first coats of primer and paint were applied. Sleek as a swan from bow to stern, the boat featured three staterooms with two restroom facilities, two showers, a spacious galley, a wet bar, a fireplace, and an electric

Hammond organ. I also requested the inclusion of a flying bridge, with controls set atop the cabin which allowed you to pilot the boat from the upper deck.

Leonard and I were in a fever to launch this splendid new vessel. By the time the boat was pronounced completed, I knew exactly what to name the craft. Always an avid reader, Violet had a particular fondness for Greek mythology. She had become enchanted by an epic poem by Ovid at the time, and suggested that we name the boat the *Galatea* after one of his alluring maidens. I commissioned the painting of two nameplates with the name *Galatea* proudly adorning them in graceful cursive letters in gray against a white background. In addition to the traditional painting of the name on the boat's stern, the nameplates were placed on prominent display on each side of the bridge.

The *Galatea* was launched at the shipyard at Santa Barbara and sailed on its maiden voyage southward along the California coast to its slip at the harbor at Long Beach, carrying eight passengers from the studio who toasted the *bon voyage*. That maiden voyage marked the beginning of nearly twenty years of happy sailing and celebration, particularly for Leonard and myself.

During many of the countless cruises of the *Galatea*. Leonard and I, of course, cherished the most intimate connection with the boat. Shipmates in many ways are like soulmates, and Leonard and I shared a fellowship on board that was so congenial in our little voyages that the vessel itself seemed to become a vibrant extension of our own personalities.

We could sense the engine and its various mechanical moods. We instinctively braced our footing to sway with the leeward or starboard motion of the craft, and we could virtually feel the distinctive, even unique temperament and maneuvering of the *Galatea* while standing on the flying bridge with a sure hand on the helm.

None of our excursions during those years ever offered any serious rivalry to the voyaging of *Kon-Tiki*. Our cruises were generally three- or four-week excursions from Long Beach, south to the warm coastal waters of Baja California. There were many times though, particularly on weekends, when we were merely content to cruise the smooth waters of Long Beach Harbor and never ventured beyond the breakwater. That's some of the most relaxing boating you can enjoy. The easy camaraderie shared with other vessel owners hailing each other from boat to boat or leisurely fishing off the stern is about the most serene recreation I can think of.

The most gratifying thing about acquiring both the Quail House and the *Galatea* was that they symbolized the continuing relationship that Violet and I had shared with her sister Vera and Leonard since those earliest years of our courtships. As identical twin sisters, Violet and Vera enjoyed a symbiotic understanding that was poignantly different from the relationships either of them had with their other siblings.

The strong similarity of our wives' temperaments provided Leonard and me with a kind of common insight into our respective mates, and intensified our own sense of kinship. Although we all spent a great deal of time together as couples, there were plenty of times when the guys and the gals played on different teams. Violet often graciously helped host many of the business parties held on board the *Galatea* for our company's agency clients, but she preferred to remain ashore. Landlubbers at heart, she and Vera were often sublimely content to visit each other at the house, where they could be engaged for hours in earnest sisterly repartee—Leonard and I donned our deck shoes and made for the harbor.

At Quail House, however, we were all at home on the range. Whether on land or sea, Violet and I were enjoying a prosperous lifestyle that neither of us had ever expected to have been blessed with.

That's not to suggest that we didn't grow happily accustomed to the lifestyle—we did. It would be incredibly coy of me to say that whatever success and affluence we'd achieved ever seemed to be an inadvertent occurrence. It never did. We both always had goals, dreams, and objectives for ourselves and our family and we'd striven, budgeted, invested, and built on those plans.

No, success and prosperity had never been an unintentional fluke. During both our formative and peak production years at the studio, I'd missed out on a lot of suppertimes, evenings, and numerous weekends or holidays with the family due to intense work demands. Through all of this Spartan striving, Violet had steadfastly upheld my commitment to the company and sacrificed uncounted hours when we could have spent time together as husband and wife and best friends.

But the exalted thing about it was that we *remained* wedded best friends throughout all of the building years. Despite many regrets, disappointments, setbacks, wins, and losses, we won and lost and grew together. Inevitably, I've grown exceedingly more mellow in recent years, and the recollection of my intense ardor for the company sometimes now gives me pause. It had indeed been a magnificent obsession, but as my wife reassures me, from her viewpoint never a malignant one.

In her own way, I think Vi is as proud of what we built—our studio, our company, and most cherished for her, our family and home—as I am. They are the miracles that have made up our lives.

I've heard it said that behind every successful man stands a woman. In my case, Violet has invariably stood *beside* me, and whatever success may be written after our names has always been a joint venture.

Chapter Fifteen

Lunch Box Heroes

Over the years we've been involved in a lot of merchandising activity which produced a large array of collectible items featuring the images of various Hanna-Barbera cartoon characters. One of the most popular items seemed to have been lunch boxes depicting the faces of Yogi Bear, The Flintstones and Dino, and The Jetsons. These characters, along with such classic live-action television competitors as The Long Ranger and The Rifleman, are often popularly referred to by memorabilia enthusiasts as "Lunch Box Heroes."

Some of those cartoon collectibles are actually on display at our studio, and they bring back a lot of memories for some of the veteran company people who remember the heydays of those series and characters. Anyone of them, including Joe and myself, can tell you that the often frenetic schedule demands and pressures involved in meeting our delivery dates exacted nothing less than heroic work efforts from our employees.

The ample array of trademarked merchandise promoting our shows are nostalgic symbols of an awesome sustained teamwork that made Hanna-Barbera the dominant cartoon studio that it was in the industry for so many years. The real "lunch box heroes" of that era are the people who shared their hard-earned noon hour breaks from 12:30 to 1:30 p.m. chewing the fat with each other along with their tuna fish, egg salad sandwiches, or pastrami and burgers off the roach coach.

Our "cartoon plant" at Hanna-Barbera has always been an informal environment. We've prided ourselves in being the kind of artistic studio that fosters creative expression and industriousness in a down-to-earth atmosphere, where dedicated folks really perform and produce on their jobs rather than merely pose in titled staff positions. I don't believe we ever imposed a dress code on our employees, and if we did, it was a lax one. People pretty much "came as they were" to work, and it might even be fair to suggest that the overall feeling at the studio among our people was almost domestic.

Despite the wide production net we threw in TV cartoon programming, the H-B lot is physically very small in size compared to the other neighboring studios in Hollywood. MGM, Disney, Paramount, and Warner are all mammoth in their acreage, and, proportionately speaking, our modest three-acre facility could easily be contained in a single corner or wing of any of those other studios.

Yet the volume of work we did during the decades of the 1960s through the 1980s was staggering. There was one season around 1979 when we were committed to producing ten shows a week. The tremendous volume of production eventually swelled the ranks of our inking and painting department alone from an initial recruitment of about twenty people to over 200 employees.

The green scrolls of exposure sheets on which I timed the direction for those shows were coming across my desk to the animators in a succession of pencil-marked paper that resembled a wire press copy machine. Artists, musicians, animators, and production managers marched in and out of my office all day.

It was, as one of our veteran production managers, Howard Hanson, used to declare, "big doings." Busy is a pygmy verb to adequately describe our peak production years. It was hectic, heartbreaking, horrendous, and I wouldn't have had it any other way.

This unbridled enthusiasm, I must admit, was not always shared by all of the troops. Although our people were for the most part proper patriots enlisted in the cause of production, Joe and I were the original fanatics in the undertaking. While Joe kept hard at it with his writers and actors conceiving the gags and cracking the jokes, I would end up cracking the whip—just for comic effect, mind you—in the production departments when there was pressure to meet air dates.

I remain hopeful that wisdom grows with age. So does benevolence, I've been assured by certain colleagues. I've certainly got the benevolent image now. Hell, at eighty-six, it's great to have any image other than one engraved in stone! It seems that I've now entered into that part of life where my white hair, grandfatherly demeanor, and encroaching kindliness all work well together to impart that benevolent image. I guess it's about time, but truth to tell, it wasn't always that way.

There were days (and plenty of nights) back then when my managerial intensity could well have won me election as tyrant of the week, month, or, more precisely, production season by a landslide of votes. There was no malevolence in this distinction, however. Everyone who worked for the company knew the pressures of the business. The only times I think that I ever really went ballistic were those critical times when foul-ups or occasional lax job performance hindered or jeopardized our ability to meet business obligations. When that happens, everybody loses.

Hardly anybody, I am convinced, who came to work at our studio and who took pride in drawing their wages ever showed up wanting to do a bad job. We all wanted to do a good job and turn out the very best animation we could. The mechanics of our overall production system were designed to allow our people to do precisely that. You have to feel your way with people, especially artists and creative personalities. The production management system that Joe and I, with our years of experience, tried to work out was an intuitive setup. We tried to alternately provide a loose tether or a tight rein appropriate to the demands of our industry's professions and its respective professionals.

Sometimes this meant hugging and sometimes this meant hollering. In general, the hugging seemed to be the preferred tactic. Personally speaking, I was easy. I could go either way. In other words, feelings may have sometimes run high but they were not meant to be hard. Admittedly, it was tougher from the "holleree's" perspective. But as the pivot man in production, the buck ultimately stopped at my desk. That was the business reality of the deal and there were times aplenty when there were a hell of a lot of bucks involved.

Pat Foley reminds me about a pet irate phrase that I often yelled as an opener when I was sore. The standard rant was, "You have just cost Hanna-Barbera a hell of a lot of money!"

Pretty blunt, I'll admit, but it got the point across. There is verity to the saying "time is money," but in production you have to elaborate on the principle. Time could convert into a *great deal of money* that was either lost or made depending on how diligently and effectively we all applied those hours to our overall work ethics.

That conviction became an adamant index of the studio's success. Still, I don't believe that any of our people will ever suggest that either Joe or I ever strove to run Hanna-Barbera as a sweat shop. That doesn't mean we didn't sweat profusely at times. In a team effort, everyone generates a lot of perspiration and inspiration, but no one generally has the time to sort out the percentages of each or is inclined to philosophize about artistic commitment. It is simply understood. To undertake what many other individuals might regard as efforts "above and beyond the call of duty," is often the work of a true professional in any calling.

Neither my partner nor I ever regarded ourselves as studio moguls, but we did tend to assume the role of concerned and often stern parents of the studio we founded. As a result, our management of Hanna-Barbera Productions evolved as a kind of democratic dictatorship which encouraged an easy informality. Friends and coworkers understood that we would all bust our tails when necessary to get our jobs done.

If there is one conviction that sixty-plus years in this business has upheld for me it is this: The one common denominator shared by everyone who loves their involvement in the cartoon industry is spirit. Talent, artistic perception, creative drive, and technical expertise can radically vary in the keenly diverse legions of people who occupy our network of production departments, season to season. That is the nature of the business. The soul of the business, however, is a singular spirit of fascination for what we do in the creation of our product. I would be greatly surprised and deeply disappointed to hear that Hanna-Barbera employees ever dismissed their work as being "just a job." What our people produced irrespective of their occupations was their own handiwork, finished with a personal touch and sometimes with a flourish.

Since I was never great shakes as an artist myself, I have a tremendous respect for people who can both color between the lines and create the line forms themselves. The alacrity with which our artists, inkers, and painters can execute the images to be animated remains for me an enduring source of admiration. It is ultimately a team effort, and it takes a legion of individual experts all harmonizing their skills to produce the cumulative result of a good picture.

Prior to the advent of photocopying, inking or outlining the sequence of scenes in a cartoon was a hands-on craft that literally employed thousands of people in the industry. A traditional inker would be given a cartoon scene to be copied in outline form on a cel, and the reproduction had to be meticulously precise.

Barbara Krueger retains vivid memories of that professional era before photocopy machines pre-empted much of the traditional hands-on inking operation of our business. During those days Barbara and other inkers would be given a scene from her supervisor to trace on a numbered cel in flawless form.

There was definitely a certain technique to the job. Inkers generally wore a cotton glove on the hand they used to draw with in order to protect the cel from oil or perspiration transfers. The inker was advised to keep their wrist stiff in order to draw a steady line and simply follow through in a smooth, fluid fashion. If the inker did make a mistake, they would generally be able to erase the error by rubbing the ink off the cel with a slender pointed wooden stick called a scraper. If they were really unhappy about how the scene was turning out—and you could have an occasional tough morning or day—the inker might discard the cel altogether and start over.

With the arrival of photocopy machines, many inking jobs were phased out: such copying machines could quickly reproduce background scenes. Joe and I issued a memorandum offering to train anyone in the inking department as assistant animators. Most of them, including Barbara, elected to take the training and most of them continued at Hanna-Barbera for many, many years.

Outside of the transition from inking to photocopying, there were no real significant technical or artistic changes in the production process within the cartoon industry. It is true that we endeavored to provide the studio with the most modern equipment possible for all our departments including editing, camera, and recording. Computers have really contributed to special effects. Even so, the industry for the most part has remained consistent over the years. Animation is still a hands-on craft, created by real people.

This consistency is affirmed by the fact that so many of our longtime employees have become "lifers" in the business. A lot of the kids who first filled out an employment form in the early days were merely applying for a temporary job. For many of them that job turned into a lifelong career, and thirty-five years later a lot of those fresh-faced youngsters are now seasoned professionals and respected veterans who grew up with the television animation industry.

Alison Leopold was a wide-eyed, long-haired, California girl who looked like she'd just stepped out of the cast of *The Brady Bunch*. Alison was a good worker from day one, but in those early years she had definite priorities shared by many young women in their early twenties. Most work in animation is seasonal and Alison, who originally occupied a small apartment almost directly across the street from the studio, would always show up promptly for work and do a great job. Despite her industriousness, it took a little while for Alison to really commit to a career. She recalls begging her supervisor in the inking and painting department, Roberta Gruder, to lay her off during the slack winter months so that she could go to the beach.

Alison continued to maintain this seasonal migration to the seashore for several years until she was eventually promoted to supervisor of the inking and painting unit. She turned out to be one of the finest department heads in our company, although I still have a good idea where I can find both her and her husband on the weekends.

Alison's pal Barbara Krueger first came to work at Hanna-Barbera with the notion of simply earning enough money to take a trip to Europe. True to her intention, Barbara worked diligently, saved her money, and at the end of the production season promptly headed for the continent to make the grand tour with her mother. The next year she was back and, like Alison, has over the years become one of the most respected and popular members of the H-B clan.

Although we had plenty of young people show up looking for employment who were as yet undecided about their futures, not everyone who applied for a job expressed such initial professional ambivalence. One of my oldest friends in the company is Star Wirth, currently the head of the studio's Xeroxing department. She originally joined our studio in 1966 as a photocopy processor. Now Star never expressed any intentions at the time of achieving any particular vocational goal with the company—although I certainly would have encouraged her to persist if she had.

What she did convey in all candor was an earnest and intense desire to work, and to keep working for as long as she could possibly hold a job. This ardent determination alone was compelling enough to command my respect and enlist my friendship. She was this young kid no more than twenty-six years old with two young daughters whose dad had run out on them. Star had no child support and no resources aside from a hell of a lot of guts and a spartan resolve to support herself and her kids.

Star has vivid memories of her executive career at Hanna-Barbera undergoing a sort of "baptism under fire." Shortly after being promoted to head of the Xeroxing department, the department was moved from the studio basement to more spacious quarters in a

Burbank office building. It was a crowded and stressful time, fraught with a lot of frantic production activity. Under these pressurized conditions, Star recalls receiving a telephone call from me in which I apparently sharply reprimanded her in high volume—and somewhat colorful language—for what I believed was some grievous supervisory oversight on her part. Now, Star was never lacking in the department of spunk. When she perceived a radical difference in our viewpoints on the situation, she let me know in no uncertain terms. A short while later when cooler heads prevailed, I realized that it was me, not she, who had been in error and called back to deliver an apology several decibels lower than my original tone.

Well, heck, anyone can make a mistake. I can tell you that I've had egg on my face that was both scrambled and easy-over, but most often and perhaps most appropriate to my executive temperament at times, *hard-boiled*. It took a lot of nerve for Star to talk up for herself. After that last exchange of fire-eaters' pyrotechnics, we formed an even stronger bond of mutual respect as friends.

One of the benefits that the Hanna-Barbera Studio produced for Joe and me was the opportunity to reunite with many of the veteran producers and animators with whom we worked back at MGM. Both Tex Avery and Friz Freleng joined us at H-B as directors of Saturday morning cartoon shows and the reunions with these guys, I'll tell you, really helped keep the creative excitement of this business as vivid for me as it was when I was a kid back at Harman-Ising, in the 1930s.

Despite failing health, Tex Avery in his last years was, in my estimation, still one of the greatest directors, storymen, and gagmen in the business. By 1979, Tex was in retirement, but Joe and I both had a hunch that Tex really wanted to go back to work. I guess we were right because Avery readily accepted our invitation that year to rejoin us, working part time at Hanna-Barbera Productions. Tex was provided an office and deferentially left to work on any project he wished. True to form, Avery displayed his exceptional flair for timing and conceiving uproariously funny gags with the creation of a cartoon pilot called *The Kwicky Koala Show*.

Joe, who was always as respectful of Tex's genius as I, loved the show, which featured an amiable and irresistibly cute Australian bear who loved to stroll through the countryside smelling the roses and snacking on eucalyptus leaves. But Kwicky's leisurely demeanor was deceptive, especially to his nemesis, Wilford Wolf, who, misled into believing Kwicky was easy prey, was stunned to find that the little koala would suddenly evade his attempts to grab him with lightning speed. This kind of gag hilarity was classic Avery comedy and always guaranteed to provoke Joe to gleeful admiration. "Tex," he recollected recently, acting out Wilford Wolf's frantic efforts to grab Kwicky, "had a gift for timing his stuff, like the *Kwicky* show, that was unique and special. It was funny as hell."

If old soldiers, according to General MacArthur, don't die, but rather fade away, aging cartoon creators often seem to just fade-out. This was true with Tex Avery, and his life closed with a haunting poignancy that contrasted ironically with the zany, rambunctious spirit of his life and work.

One summer afternoon in 1980, I drove onto the studio lot and found Tex sitting on the concrete steps that led to the rear entry of the administration building. I was stunned at how physically diminished he appeared. His face was frightfully pale and there was a look of apprehension, actually open fear, that suddenly chilled me despite the July heat. "Tex," I said with alarm, "you're not well, are you?"

My old friend and mentor looked up at me with eyes that were pathetically childlike in their bewilderment. "No, Bill," he whispered, "but I figured that if I sat here, you'd find me and take care of me."

Somehow, I managed to get Tex into my car and drove him to St. Joseph's Hospital in the San Fernando Valley, where I was told by his physicians that Tex was suffering from terminal cancer. This was a devastating blow. I believe that Tex knew that he was dying but he wasn't ready to go, and none of us who were his friends were ready to let him go either. Gamely, he continued to talk about plans of going back to work at the studio and resuming work on his latest cartoon project.

During the last few remaining weeks of his life, Tex was visited at his hospital bed by a continuous procession of friends and colleagues, including Joe Barbera and myself. It was a time of great anguish, not only for Joe and me, but for the studio and our entire industry as we watched with helpless sorrow Avery's life ebb away in those last few days. An incredulous assembly of animators, artists, writers, and other professional comrades reluctantly resigned themselves to Tex Avery's passing.

I found myself wrapped in a melancholic reverie, as memories of open-hearted hilarity enjoyed with Tex on fishing and camping trips, boating excursions, and even the mischievous ribaldry of our early carpooling days to work at MGM came back to me like echoes and reflections of happier times.

The end finally came for Tex on August 26, 1980. He was seventy-two years old. It marked not only the passing of a great pioneer in animation, but for me, symbolized the passing of an era.

The late Friz Freleng was another legendary innovator in early animation who was happily reunited with us at Hanna-Barbera. He joined us in 1983 to work on the development of the cartoon series *Pink Panther and Sons*, a series based on the famous pastel-colored feline originally created by Friz. A lot of footage had gone through the projectors since the days when Friz and I had worked with rather disgruntled diligence on the old Captain and the Kids pictures during that period pretty much characterized by Joe Barbera and me as "BTJ" ("Before Tom and Jerry"). Having Friz on the lot helped bring back memories of the callow excitement of those sophomore years. Despite the fact that he was pushing eighty around then, Friz was still one of the best animation directors in the industry. He was with us at H-B for two years, and only recently passed away in 1995.

Our company was exceedingly fortunate in retaining a rich alumni of animators as well. Both Ray Patterson and Irv Spence were MGM veterans who joined us as part of our original staff when we formed Hanna-Barbera. They continued to work for many years for us as key animators who basically showed their reverent younger colleagues how it was done.

Spence and Patterson have since retired from the business, but friendships with guys like them are not the kind that you allow to drift into forgetfulness. During the past several years, a group of surviving longtime colleagues, including Ray and Irv, has retained a stubborn tradition of meeting once a month at a favorite Hollywood restaurant for lunch. There at our monthly reunions, Irv Spence, Ray Patterson, Carl Urbano, Art Scott, Don Lusk, and myself indulge ourselves in the kind of raucous raconteuring peculiar to aging animators. Sixty-five years of comradeship covers a lot of cartooning, and it proved to be a real character-building experience for all of us. I'm sorry to say that Irv recently passed away in the autumn of 1995, although I know he's there in spirit.

Inevitably, many of our fondest recollections are retreads of anecdotes we've swapped and have become nearly endless in their retellings. Who the hell cares? There are some things that are really worth living and even some, when you have enough history behind you, that are preciously worth re-living again and again. That may admittedly be the partisan assertion of a die-hard cartoon producer. It is an automatic reflex now to rerun the reels and review the frames and images as they once were and should have been.

The truth of it is that for me, these memories that feature in starring roles all the lunch box heroes of Hanna-Barbera may be the greatest animated action production of all times.

Chapter Sixteen

Foreign Exchanges

With all due reverence for that venerable firefighter Smokey and other celebrity bruins, I think I can say with a fair degree of confidence that Yogi Bear is probably the most famous bear in the world. Yogi has become an icon, and his image and antics have been broadcast in cartoon shows all over the world and dubbed into a multitude of languages. Of course, this also has been true of many of our other cartoon series, but Yogi's international fame seems particularly symbolic to me of the universal appeal of cartoon entertainment.

With this growing magnitude of global popularity, it was perhaps inevitable that the economic as well as the entertainment influence of the animation industry would eventually resonate throughout the world. By the end of the 1970s, the Hanna-Barbera studio had earned the distinction of being the largest producer of cartoons in the industry. The gross and net earnings from cartoon sales as well as merchandising transactions were huge, and compelled the employment of an immense and varied network of employees and business affiliates.

Our facilities had become extended to the bursting point. We literally had every available qualified animator in town busily engaged in some production or another. Joe and I had seen this coming for some time. For years we'd maintained a frenetic pace of production and business development as our studio and company had thrived along with the industry we had fostered. But now events had reached a point where the animation business had, in true cartoon fashion, become like the orphaned elephant that threatened to outgrow the house of its adoptive parents.

Expansion was clearly imminent. We would simply have to build a bigger house for the critter. In order to do that effectively, we would have to go farther than across town. The largest expanse of elbow room that beckoned was in fact waiting for us overseas.

A huge amount of the amazing acceleration of our business of course, must be credited to Joe Barbera's remarkable aptitude for initiating the creative development of a phenomenal succession of great cartoon show concepts and his distinct flair for selling them. We had a lot on our plate in terms of meeting delivery dates for an abundance of orders for Hanna-Barbera cartoon shows. Talk about prosperity programs! Not only were our plates heaped high, but our cups were running over.

While it was Joe who generated the sales, it was me who had to deliver the shows. Over the years I had striven to organize the production end of our company into an organic phalanx that could effectively operate at both maximum creative and technical efficiency.

We had a wide and diverse corps of people who required constant encouragement, direction, and management to sustain our many production endeavors. In order to achieve this, you had to know what your people were capable of doing both as individuals and as part of a larger unit. Sometimes those capabilities had a tendency to work against themselves if contention involving supervision or organizational problems developed within the studio's units.

With the complexity of individual operational deadlines, respective departmental priorities, artistic differences, and other creative and technical elements involved in running a studio, I often felt we had the proverbial "tiger by the tail." There are ways, however, to tame the beast.

The primary key to making any enterprise work is communication. You have to be able to talk with your people. No one ever ran a successful business by having a bunch of folks sitting around second-guessing each other. Early on in the formation of our company, Joe and I began a tradition of consistently keeping each other apprised of our respective professional obligations, creative perspectives, and individual administrative concerns.

As our company grew, this mutual advisement expanded to a communicative fellowship involving everyone working for the studio. As a company, we prided ourselves on being an ambitious professional organism that had been able to hang onto its humanity over the years.

Frequently nowadays, I'll go out to lunch with some old colleague or retired employee and reminisce over the hectic times of the past. Now and again one of these friends will nudge the nostalgic a little with some remark like: "With you as boss, Bill, it was always a give-and-take situation. You gave the orders and we took them." Never disarmed by such comradely banter, I would generally quip back: "I always thought it was the other way around." The truth of the matter was that we had a very flexible system of operation at the studio.

I had complete faith that everyone from the mailroom to management not only knew their own jobs, but were exceptionally trained in their ability to efficiently interact with other departments when necessary to function as coordinated units.

Such alacrity simply could not exist in a rigidly structured program of operation. The ceaseless demands and implacable delivery deadlines imposed on everyone for what proved to be more than two decades of peak volume production generated enough stress. We didn't need restrictive policies that dictated how our folks should do their jobs.

Artists, writers, and other creative professionals require a reasonable latitude for individual expression if you really want to receive their loyalty as well as talent. This doesn't necessarily mean that you treat them with kid gloves. But it is critical that you provide these folks with the kinds of professional guidelines that create channels for their creativity rather than walls against this initiative.

This basic professional respect also extends in a somewhat different form to other personnel whose professional functions are definitely more technical than artistic. Tracers, inkers, clerical people, cameramen, and janitors all provided an invaluable contribution to the overall professional quality of the studio's operation and warranted their own proper degree of occupational sovereignty.

I had worked long enough in the business to believe that you can virtually do it all—if you don't try to do it all alone. This realization had its genesis back at MGM when Joe and I first teamed together, and the spirit of such units as ours eventually helped spawn the constant growth of specialized and aligned units that emerged as the TV cartoon industry.

The business survived and thrived because it was in essence a mastermind alliance that contained within it the combined intelligence and creative energy of every professional citizen of the animation industry. The implacable challenge of creative management is not only to endeavor to initiate that intelligence and energy, but to harness and direct it as well. I am convinced that the real challenge of any entrepreneur worth their salt is to realize their endeavors by expanding their dreams to embrace the aspirations of others.

What this fundamentally translates into in business is the creation of jobs and career opportunities. A retired inker once described Hanna-Barbera to me as "the biggest employment agency in the cartoon business." That is not a greatly exaggerated statement.

Given the seasonal nature of many of the jobs in our industry, we had a lot of people coming to us year after year applying for and getting work. There's a lot of free-lancing that goes on in this business, and thousands of inkers, painters, animators, film editors, and even writers and producers have generally accepted the migratory nature of their professional involvement in the animation industry as traditional and a way of life.

During the 1970s, however, we were all up to our ears in work. We were virtually beating the bushes to come up with enough qualified personnel to make our deliveries. In production, time is as vital a commodity as skilled talent and I could see that we could be faced with a critical shortage of both if we didn't come up with some way of developing additional facilities manned by qualified personnel.

From the first year or so of our company's formation, representatives from various small studios abroad had approached us about contracting work from us to produce animation footage for both theatrical and commercial use. We had at first declined these early overtures, but as production demands grew over the years, we gradually availed ourselves of contracting certain foreign companies to undertake a portion of production work commissioned as payment on a per-foot basis of animation.

Our gradual expansion into foreign production had proven to be an effective and viable aspect of our overall operation. We maintained business connections with small studios in Taipei, Madrid, Mexico, and Australia. Initially all of these studios operated as very small companies with limited facilities. But they were all staffed by qualified animators, background artists, and layout people who augmented our work force while allowing us to circumvent the time-consuming process of having to orient and educate untrained employees.

In 1957, the animation industry had been confronted with the necessity of either adapting its form to the vehicle of television and creating a market for its product in that medium, or becoming extinct. That market had burgeoned beyond any of our wildest projections. A dozen years later, those of us who had fostered the industry were challenged with just as critical a need to develop, on a massive level, the production facilities and personnel essential to meet what had become an almost overwhelming demand for that very product.

Producing television cartoons had become a mammoth business. But business and industry are distinctly different things when it comes to supply and demand. The *industry* supplies the demand which generates the *business*. The industry, in fact, needs the business in order to survive, but there has to be a symmetry and balance in their relationship. It's wonderful to have people clamoring for your product as long as you don't go broke in the process of trying to fill your orders. Free enterprise is a marvelous system, but it is also a tightrope. It is just as easy for a company to be consumed by the soaring production costs and overhead incurred from over-extending their capacity to meet a swelling demand as it is to confront the financial ruin of market famine.

During the 1970s, Hanna-Barbera as well as other cartoon studios had a bonanza of business beckoning to us like the mother lode if we could effectively handle the production and delivery. We were all doing the best we could, but there were times when my production staff felt more besieged by the business than blessed. I looked long and hard at the logistical challenges of all this immense business acceleration. After some discussions with Joe and some intense calculation and pondering, we came to the inescapable conclusion that a decisive and directed expansion of overseas operation for our company was absolutely essential.

Our previous professional affiliations with the companies we'd contracted abroad had been amenable and productive. The artists and animators overseas merged well with the overall production system at Hanna-Barbera, and the revenues generated by foreign affiliates from their contracts with us had in some instances subsidized the germination of animation production as an international industry. There were, I was convinced, fertile fields abroad for the flourishing of this industry and Hanna-Barbera—if we could set up and develop our own foreign network of studios and extend the boundaries of commercial cartoonmaking throughout the world.

After an initial evaluation of prospective locations for such expansion, we concluded that Australia would be a good place to start. Although we were prepared to work with any communication problems that might arise from language differences, it was just common sense to launch the organization of our first foreign studio in a country that spoke English.

I was absolutely confident of my ability and experience in putting a cartoon studio together, but assimilating people of different cultures to the logistics of our American operations would still be a trial-and-error process. If I was going to break ground in this region of business development, I preferred to do it without an interpreter.

I also had a great respect for the intrinsic intelligence and industriousness of Aussies as a people. This fundamental respect on my part was to prove well grounded by the production colleagueship that flourished with our Australian alliance in the years to come.

In 1971, we contracted to produce a cartoon series for ABC called *The Funky Phantom*, which I decided would be the premier vehicle to launch our foreign production of cartoon series in Australia. We were totally inundated with work at our California studio and the only way we could deliver the show would be to produce it abroad.

Accordingly, Violet and I booked a flight to Sydney to scout out the various facilities and meet some of the folks currently involved in Australian animation production. During this reconnaissance, I became impressed with some layouts by a talented animator named Zoran Janjic. After some discussion with Zoran, I was convinced that I had found the right guy to function as manager of the Australian studio—to be called Hanna-Barbera Australia.

Setting up our first major production facility there proved to be an entirely novel adventure. The core staff we recruited was a group of about sixty young people who were as congenial a gathering of folks you'd ever want to meet. They were a fun bunch of kids, and Vi and I had good times hosting a series of in-house picnics and get-togethers during the weeks we all spent working together to set up their studio. Despite their youth, all of these people were experienced in animation production—respective of their abilities, of course—and the initial organization of the studio was a fairly seamless operation. By spring, we were up to speed and production was underway.

By 1977, our company employed approximately 2,000 people and was turning out 10,000 feet of processed film a week for broadcast. That translated to the production of about eight half-hour shows a week. This staggering program demand by the networks and syndicate stations was still growing at an awesome rate.

The production proficiency of our Australian units proved to be so efficacious to our overall operations that it set the pattern for the eventual development of satellite studios all over the world.

In commencing a campaign for the global development of Hanna-Barbera production organs, I knew that I'd have to be prepared to embark on long and extended absences from our home studio. This did not particularly worry me, for I had great confidence in the overall efficiency of our system of operation, but I did feel a responsibility to delegate the production management of the company to sure and capable hands. Joe had his own hands just as full with our company's creative and business development. But there was another Barbera on the company payroll who I was convinced possessed all of the drive and potential to efficiently oversee the studio's production during my absences abroad.

Joe's daughter Jayne had inherited her dad's ambition, intelligence, and natural charm to a remarkable degree. In addition, Jayne was also very much her own person, a distinctly self-realized young woman with exceptional organizational aptitude and administrative poise.

Jayne and I had built our careers in the animation business in very similar ways. We had both started in an inking and painting unit and worked our way up to head the department. The major difference between our supervisory responsibilities in this area was that in my day, the roster of employees I directed at Harman-Ising seldom exceeded more than twenty, while the unit that Jayne managed at Hanna-Barbera numbered more than 200 people. That was about three times as many employees as the entire staff of Harman-Ising, and the volume of work handled by Jayne's department was tremendously greater than what we'd ever done at Hugh and Rudy's studio.

Bringing Jayne up to speed as production manager was a relatively easy process. The logistics of running her inking and painting department were very similar to the supervisory challenge of managing the studio. The overall scope of this management was of course much greater, but Jayne had grown up with the business and I had complete confidence in both her intuitive and practical grasp of our system.

To give you an idea of the constellation of responsibilities entrusted to Jayne during my absence, a brief "crash course" of our studio's basic method of operation might give a clearer picture of how our system functioned.

It all commenced with the almighty sale. Our company received the delivery date from the network specifying when a certain amount of shows must be aired. The production manager then made a production schedule with a weekly agenda of deadlines for each department calculated upon what must be produced on a week-to-week basis to meet the delivery date.

Each department head was required to make out a production report, which was then submitted in weekly production meetings to monitor the individual progress of each department. If a department was falling behind in delivering their quota of either scripts or production for that weekly deadline (and this was a constant concern and factor), adjustments had to be made immediately to accelerate the work in that particular department to maintain the schedule.

That was the functioning nature of our industry in a nutshell. Saying is one thing, however, and doing is quite another. These principles may appear to be cogent and precise in their written form but that description can belie the exhaustive and often frenetic demands loaded to the extreme upon every unit in the system.

Jayne took over the duties of production manager in 1977, right in the teeth of our peak production season. It was a tremendous responsibility for a young woman to carry in what was then, quite frankly, a male-dominated industry. But Jayne, in addition to her keen intellect and spartan discipline, had spirit. She had the heart as well as the mind for the job, and I was proud and confident to have her on the bridge.

My own sense of professional responsibility compelled me to maintain a constant—and I mean nearly ceaseless—communication by telephone with Jayne to keep me apprised of the daily production status of the studio while I was abroad. Passing the torch of leadership is one thing, but passing the buck is another. I'd delegated heavy authority and formidable duties to an exceptional adjutant, but I felt that it was still up to me to provide Jayne Barbera with the administrative guidance and support necessary to sustain an effective aligned leadership of the studio.

Knowing that the piloting of our studio would be in Jayne's capable hands imparted me with a certain peace of mind. That was about the only thing peaceful that I recall about that period of time in our industry. The idea of sending some of our footage to be produced abroad met with some stiff opposition by a large number of union production people in our company who felt that such a move threatened their own jobs.

This ember of discontent was eventually fanned from disgruntled complaints into a full-blown strike at Hanna-Barbera in 1977. Picket lines formed and arrays of placards and signs were displayed by inkers, painters, animators, and artists who declaimed their objections to foreign production.

From the viewpoint of the management, it should be realized that none of us ever intended or believed that expanding our operations abroad would deprive our own people here in the U.S. of a livelihood. Business was flourishing at that time here, and there was more than enough work for everyone, not only at Hanna-Barbera but within the entire cartoon industry itself. Disney was busy, Warner was busy, and our combined production demands had, if anything, dramatically accelerated general employment opportunities in the animation business.

The dilemma for management was that such fluctuation often put us in a real bind whenever we received a large order of shows while understaffed. Other studios had often already hired all the available animators and other production people. On the other side of the coin and for that matter the ocean, we had been receiving for years overtures from numerous foreign animation studios who were crying for work, as well as offering attractive costs. It seemed a fair and effective alternative.

Through the international distribution of our cartoons, we had gained a worldwide audience for our product and enjoyed immense revenues from those foreign sales. As far as I was concerned, it seemed only fair that as long as there was enough work for our own people here, we should allow other countries who had become our customers an opportunity to share in the commercial benefits of being involved in the production end of the business as well.

There was a growing number of small animation studios abroad that had been turning out commercials or theatrical cartoons for several years, hoping to expand the scope of their operations into producing cartoons for television. Many of them were staffed by eminently qualified animators and artists who knew their professions as well as any of our folks here. It was clear to me—and I was convinced to many other veterans of the business—that the commercial convulsions emanating from the controversy of this strike were in reality the growing pains of a business destined to expand into an international industry.

Fortunately, the strike proved to be relatively short-lived. Arbitration ultimately concluded that producers were contractually unrestricted by their relations with unions in determining where production was to be done.

Responding to the now undeniable blockbuster popularity of animation entertainment, our flagship company was compelled to "turn it loose" so to speak, and commit to an ambitious campaign of amplifying our industry to global proportions. During the next fifteen years I was to find myself constantly en route upon what ultimately proved to be a commercial itinerary involving the development of production facilities or studios in countries including China, Spain, Argentina, Mexico, the Philippines, and Poland.

This international network of operations not only expedited the volume of production but generally enhanced the quality of the product itself as well. Each studio in every country was organized to provide a varied array of production functions respective to their size and scope of operation. Some of the larger studios, such as the one in Taipei organized in alliance between myself and a brilliant young producer named James Wang, were completely self-contained facilities that were equipped and staffed to handle the entire spectrum of cartoon production. On the other hand, we also had numerous affiliates in several other countries, including Mexico, with units set up to function in only certain specified aspects of production, such as inking and painting.

Whatever the proportion of production these companies embraced, the overall system to which each contributed nourished an effective relay system of "foreign exchange." It not only expedited and expanded our entire industrial operation, but fostered new fields of world commerce as well.

I am no foreign diplomat, but my extended circuit of international travel conducted for the purpose of establishing these production enclaves convinced me of one belief. There are few things that can promote international goodwill more than the advancement of free enterprise. Human understanding is a quality and ideal that moves from the abstract to active realization when folks develop that understanding through the active involvement of something they all have in common and believe in. Any new H-B studio wasn't just an impersonal production unit. No, each had its identity and each entered into the spirit of their creations—as well as forging a professional and personal bond to its parent company.

The development of such enterprises were in many ways as unique as the nations in which they were fostered. Yet they all had two things distinctly in common. Wherever I went, I found that the people we engaged to work with us loved both their involvement in a team effort and the prospect of learning or extending their creative and professional skills.

James Wang was a young producer with a mild-mannered, almost self-effacing manner that belied an intense entrepreneurial drive to succeed in the cartoon business. While still in his twenties, James had formed his own production studio in a garage in Taipei, hoping to secure production contracts from such American animation studios as Disney and Warner.

To his dismay, none of them would see him on his initial visit to the U.S., and I remember seeing a touching mixture of dejection and determination on Wang's face when he first walked into my office.

By the time James walked out of my office, we had a gentlemen's agreement that he would be engaged to provide production services to Hanna-Barbera as our show sales warranted. That was the beginning of a professional alliance that has lasted over twenty years. During those two decades, James Wang has developed that first embryonic studio into a flourishing company that has employed more than 600 people. Horatio Alger would have doffed his hat.

In working with people all over the world, I discovered an egalitarian enthusiasm that had no boundaries and created its own democracy within any and all geographical borders. I always loved working right alongside everyone in our crew regardless of where I was. It was always a hands-on, team effort from storyboards to putting the scissors to the last foot of film.

It didn't take long for anyone recruited in such enterprise to become zealots possessed of that magnificent obsession called "delivery." When schedules became strained to the bursting point and production demands tyrannical, it was not uncommon to find artists and animators sharing common quarters in whatever house or apartment Vi and I might have leased, grabbing catnaps on sleeping bags as we all doggedly punched away in marathon exertions to meet our deadlines.

The nerve center of all this industry, of course, was our flagship studio in Hollywood. Jayne Barbera was doing an exceptional job of production management at home. The efficiency with which all our units there were operating made my heart swell with a pride that was downright paternal.

Despite the undeniably phenomenal success we enjoyed from this foreign exchange program of a global production network, the system was not infallible. Foreign production could be a real circus of frenzied performances, characterized by an ample share of juggling acts, tightrope walks, and balancing feats involving maintaining quality control and monitoring the schedule quotas of every aspect and unit of international operation.

Things could and often did go wrong, threatening in their malfunction disastrous consequences. The worst possible scenario in production is failure to make an air date. In effect, we would have failed to hold up our end of a contract to the network to deliver. That would have meant not only a loss of face, but the forfeit of a tremendous amount of money as well.

Fortunately, this has never happened at Hanna-Barbera. But there were times, as many of my colleagues will attest, that we came pretty damned close. In retrospect, some of these crises, as dire as they were at the time, were often characterized by a perverse hilarity that left us not knowing whether to laugh or cry.

One particularly perplexing event which precisely exemplifies how we could sometimes be "ambushed" by confusion was recalled to me recently by a close friend named Margaret Loesch, who is currently the president of the Fox Children's Network. Joe and I first met Margaret while she was serving as a network executive in children's programming at NBC and were vividly impressed by her remarkable administrative capabilities. She was obviously a comer in the business and we both knew it.

I became convinced that Margaret could be an invaluable administrative ally in our push for foreign production if she could be persuaded to join us at Hanna-Barbera. "If you ever get antsy at the network," I repeatedly suggested to her, "consider coming over and working for us."

Margaret eventually joined us in 1979 as Vice-President of Children's Programs at Hanna-Barbera. Her job was initially to supervise a staff of writers, develop new programs, sell the programs, get them on the air, and act as a liaison between our company and the client.

It was a lot of responsibility that could have proved overwhelming to many other executives, regardless of their abilities and experience. But Margaret rose to the challenges magnificently. She remembers one particular occasion when a certain faux pas had her totally confounded.

Now, in addition to her sterling executive talents, Margaret is also a born storyteller, so I'll let her tell this little episode in her own way.

"We were doing this animated show for NBC called *The Gary Coleman Show*, and the network in its typical fashion had picked it up at the very last minute. Of course, we couldn't turn down a sale, it was paying the paycheck. So I pushed it and Joe Barbera pushed it, and all the time Bill, you were hollering, 'What are you doing? Can't you get them to delay the air date?' Well, of course, I couldn't get them to delay the air date, and you just had to do it!

"The next thing I knew, you had a unit going in Mexico. God help us! I was very nervous about this. It was a totally untried unit and I felt very insecure about it.

"When the footage came back, I got a call from Pat Foley in editing. 'Margaret, you'd better come down here. We've got a rough assembly of the *Gary Coleman* footage. *You'd better come down here.*'

"My heart sank at the tone. 'How bad is it?' I asked. 'Pretty bad. *As a matter of fact, I don't think I've ever seen worse!*'

Of course, Gary Coleman was a huge hit on NBC [on *Different Strokes*]. He was a very important star. After looking at the footage I remember calling you with the bad news. 'Bill, we have a problem. This stuff looks awful!' You were undaunted. 'Oh, it couldn't be that bad. A few cuts here, a few cuts there. We'll have it fixed up.'

"Well, Bill, you were undaunted but I was unconvinced. 'Bill!' I finally screamed. 'They've drawn Gary Coleman as white!'"

Fortunately, we were able to make all the appropriate adjustments, but it just goes to show you that creative dilemmas can come in a variety of complexions.

By 1985, Hanna-Barbera had developed a global alliance of eight countries turning out over 100 half-hour cartoon shows for the season.

In the way of things taking their own inevitable course, it was not the *sky* that had proven to be the limit for the animation industry, but the *world*. Or are there any limits at all to such a fanciful business? At any rate the possibility occurred to me that with the advent of worldwide production and distribution, an industry had come of age.

I would have handed out cigars except that I'd quit smoking. Still, the conclusion of nearly two decades of hustling all over the globe carrying the cartoon banner to new patriots seemed to merit some kind of personal milestone. The realization of this gave me pause.

Sitting in my Taipei hotel room one afternoon, I found myself in a strange reverie. The signs and billboards lettered in Chinese just outside my window reminded me of the growing array of our cartoon shows that were now being dubbed in foreign languages. They seemed to emphasize in yet another way the growing universality of the animation industry.

It was a realization that brought me no small measure of satisfaction. Yet I felt oddly discontented and restless. Well, we'd finished up another production season in good form, and there was good reason and a number of ways to celebrate. I considered the matter a little longer and then began making some phone calls. In my heart there was no doubt now of what I wanted to do. I wanted to go home.

Chapter Seventeen

Stock Footage

Hannas have always been a hearty clan. My parents were exceptionally healthy people and had long and active lives. I was fortunate to have inherited the vigorous genes from both sides of the family and was undeniably getting a lot of mileage out of them.

This did not mean that I took my longevity for granted. I always tried to take care of myself and disciplined myself to the routine of regular medical checkups. Everything had always appeared to be functioning as it should. All seemed well, or so I thought.

One morning in 1990, after completing a treadmill exercise at St. Joseph Medical Center, my physician approached me with a clipboard and a concerned frown. Now, physician's frowns, as we all know, are ominous things.

"We have a problem, Bill," he said in an almost apologetic tone. *We?* I thought. *That's my chart he's got. What is this "we" reasoning?*

"Well, doctor," I managed to reply. "What is *our* problem?"

The doctor's face looked grave. Well, maybe that's not the best choice of words. What I was told in essence was that my arteries, due to excessive blockage, were not pumping an adequate supply of blood. I was in critical need of a bypass operation.

"Geez!" I thought. I felt great or so I believed. I was assured by my physician that following the procedure, I would feel a hell of a lot better.

The remarkably swift recovery rate from such heart surgery has been documented by so many other patients that a personal description of my own rapid recuperation might seem trite. But there is nothing at all trivial about the profound impact that such surgery can have upon the psyche of anyone who has undergone such an experience.

The expression "open your heart to others" is primarily meant to be a metaphoric statement encouraging emotional accessibility. It is a jarringly different matter when the admonition is taken literally.

The heart, if you'll forgive the pun, is a tender subject. Throughout all the years I'd written poetry, I'd often referred to it as a traditional symbol of romance and love represented in form by the traditional design of a valentine. During the countless invocations at Boy Scout meetings I'd participated in, we'd ceremoniously placed our hands over our hearts and pledged our allegiance to the American flag. All of those emotional experiences and rituals had always been heartfelt. I would feel the throbbing, the pride, the affection, and the love.

But until my surgery, the heart had always been, for me, a private refuge, inviolable and invulnerable. All of that changed following the surgery. In order to ensure its survival, my heart had been invaded, incised, and then repaired. And through this experience, personal perceptions were challenged and in some ways altered dramatically. The heart was no longer a remote symbolic seat of emotions. It was also, I realized with a new immediate intensity, the vital physical pump of my life's blood. This was a jarring contrast to the metaphoric heart of emotional abstracts, and my recognition of this led to a profound sense of humility.

Alongside the emotional and spiritual growth that I liked to believe my heart had acquired during seven decades of living, that same heart had also suffered a toll from the cumulative wear and tear of life's stress.

Following my procedure, I allowed for a week's recovery. Then I returned to work and embarked on a convalescence that not only led to physical recovery, but perhaps even more importantly, a gradual emotional enlightenment.

Opening my heart had in some ways opened my mind as well. Gradually I began to consider that the emotional and physical energies that issue from the heart are perhaps in essence the same. The heart as symbol and as dynamic organ is a miracle of functioning balance in the human experience. It is no mere coincidence that the words health and harmony begin with the same letter as the word heart.

My eldest granddaughter Laurie, who is now a beautiful grown woman, has often described our family as "heart people." In the past, I'd often read that to be a reference to the commonality we all shared as emotional and sentimental individuals. In recent years, though, I've come to believe that Laurie's trusting, childlike conviction that we should follow our hearts in life, had a precocious wisdom of its own. In following our hearts we can healthily, wisely, and faithfully align ourselves with the essential life force within us and be empowered in body, mind, and spirit.

These thoughts did not come as sudden revelations but rather as a growing awareness. The vivid confrontation of one's own mortality can lead a fellow to ponder if he's going to be around long enough to glean any genuine understanding of why he was put on this earth in the first place.

I had been blessed throughout my life with exceptionally good health. This despite the fact that I have always been somewhat accident-prone, managing somehow to survive a near Guinness record for sustaining cuts, bruises, stumbles, and pratfalls over the years. Perhaps appropriate to the spirit of my industry, I have always been impulsive, spontaneous, and often headstrong in my general approach to living. Life was a buoyant Boy Scout adventure and I was prepared to enjoy it.

This exuberance found infinitely greater release when I married Vi. Violet brought to my life an amazing, endearing, earnest, spiritual incentive that taught me the profundity of existence. Violet has not only been a staunch supporter of my career, she has been a devout patriot. This dedication is exceeded only by her iron devotion to our family and friends. Her indomitable feminine strength is about as close as anything I've ever seen to the literal manifestation of the term "velvet steamroller."

If there is a distinctively consistent element in the Hanna family tradition, it is a commonly held love of poetry. This had its roots in the literary endeavors of my mother and sisters. It's something I've shared with my wife and has been passed down to our children and grandchildren as well.

If I am a casual scribbler of verses, Violet is a passionate reader of poetry. My wife loves all kinds of poetry and it doesn't matter to her whether the verses were composed by Shakespeare or Shelley or are the heartfelt work of some obscure scribe. Violet finds comfort, encouragement and loveliness in certain verses, and her appreciation of poetry is intensely personal and entirely uninfluenced by literary vogue. One of her greatest joys throughout our marriage has been to share, by reading aloud to me, some luminous passage that almost invariably gives me pause to consider the often elusive serene simplicity of life.

Ambition is great, and I've always gone through life with a full head of steam. But there is a fundamental poise in living that we are all challenged to acquire, lest all the sound and fury of it signify nothing.

One particular favorite of Violet's that I've always felt eloquently expressed this wisdom is "The Day Is Done" by Henry Wadsworth Longfellow. The following passages hold an especially personal significance for me:

> Come, read to me some poem,
> Some simple and heartfelt lay,
> That shall soothe this restless feeling,
> And banish the thoughts of day.
>
> Not from the grand old masters,
> Not from the bards sublime,
> Whose distant footsteps echo
> Through the corridors of Time.
>
> Such songs have power to quiet
> The restless pulse of care,
> And come like the benediction
> That follows after prayer.

* * *

Having entered what many people might regard as the "elder statesman" era of our careers, neither Joe nor I have ever seriously entertained any thought of retirement. Both of us continue to show up for work nearly every day: our two cars can reliably be found parked side by side, with the two of us occupying our own individual offices in close proximity with each other since the studio's inception. Following the sale to Taft, our studio was acquired in 1989 by Great American Broadcasting Company. In 1991, the regime shifted once again when Hanna-Barbera was purchased by Turner Broadcasting Company. This latest acquisition signaled to me the initiation of a new guard for Hanna-Barbera Productions with the naming of Fred Seibert as president while Joe and I were accorded the titles of Co-Chairmen and Co-Founders.

In recent years, my partner and I have happily worked on our respective projects, including producing our own television cartoon shorts and various writing projects. Joe has taken Hanna-Barbera into live-action, with dramas made for television. In 1989, however, we had an opportunity to collaborate in the production of the full-length animated feature *Jetsons, The Movie*.

It was a joyous and completely hands-on project for us. Joe and I worked as closely together on the film as we had on any of the first shows we produced during the early years of our partnership. A movieola was set up for us in a room on the second floor of the administration building and the two of us supervised the editing of virtually every foot of film that came in from dailies. Released on July 6, 1990 by Universal Pictures, the film proved popular—a nice change from the Jetsons' initial experience as a primetime cartoon almost thirty years before.

Having bid fond adieu to the Jetsons in their big screen orbit, Joe and I felt that a similar cinematic tribute to the Flintstones was due—an appropriately symmetrical finale to our other timeless primetime family. As we pondered this, my partner and I were thrilled, and somewhat astonished, to receive a proposal from Steven Spielburg and his production company, Amblin Entertainment, Inc., to do a live-action motion picture featuring our modern stone age family. This film, in association with Universal, and for which Joe and I would serve as co-producers, was to be titled (guess what?) *The Flintstones*.

Collaborating as an advisor on a film adapting such recognizable animated characters to live-action performances proved to be a unique career experience. It also provided me with my one (and only) role as an actor in a feature film. Well, "role" might be a stretch. In reality it was a cameo and my fifteen minutes of fame as an actor was actually clocked down to about fifteen seconds on the screen. My experience gave me a new appreciation of what professional actors go through. I drove up to the studio at about seven o'clock in the morning and went through make-up and wardrobe just like any other cast member.

Appropriately garbed in animal skins (which I believe were actually "cruelty-free" synthetics), I went to the set and shook hands with John Goodman, with whom I would be appearing in a boardroom scene. This scene took nearly all day to film. Goodman, by the way, did a splendid job of capturing the blustery essence of Fred Flintstone—certainly it was a challenge taking on an *animated* character whose personality has been familiar to fans for more than thirty years.

Joe and I attended the film's premiere in New York in the fall of 1994. Confidentially folks, it gives one pause to see your own face blown up to the size of a Buick on the screen! Shaving will never be the same for me again. Still, the whole experience was great fun.

Jetsons: The Movie proved to be our swan song as a collaborative production team, and both films of Hanna-Barbera's favorite two families marked a happy finale to more than fifty years of a fruitful, often frantic, and always eventful career in animation production.

* * *

During the course of working on this book, I've taken the opportunity on numerous occasions to run a variety of old home movies, as well as various promotional video clips of our company, to sharpen my recollection of past events. I've watched the images of my wife as a young mother, my mother and father as indulgent grandparents, and my son and daughter as precocious kids, come alive again with vivid poignancy.

There too, before me, are the pictures of Joe Barbera and myself along with battalions of colleagues and coworkers giving the performances of our lives in an ongoing production that spans over fifty years.

It is inevitable that a guy who has produced as much film as I have would eventually come to regard the word "footage" as a metaphor for a primary life's experience.

Footage, in retrospect, has come to mean the memories of a sequence of life's episodes that has turned out to be the most wonderful production of all. Seeing and remembering it once again has allowed me to take stock of what some of it was all about and perhaps in some ways could have been. From scene to scene, story to story, the script was pretty much written day to day in what has added up to be a very long life. It may not add up to an epic, but it has for me turned out to be a great series. But then, I've been blessed with an exceptional cast.

Epilogue:
Titles and Credits

The bookends enclosing the opening and closing of any cartoon are called titles and credits. Those are the brief chronicles—the fleeting prologues and epilogues—that identify a production and acknowledge the people involved in its creation.

What bonds these two components together is the work itself, and this axiom to me is a durable example of how art imitates life. A poet once wrote that "work is love made evident." The experience of walking, working, weeping, laughing, and sometimes hollering has taught me that the same is true of life itself.

Magic (and yes, Virginia, there is such a thing) exists in both life and art. The adventure, fun, and the challenge of our work in life is the job of discovering, experiencing, and expressing that magic. That is our divine assignment as producers in life.

As I've mentioned before, the creation of a cartoon is an alchemy that is intended to evoke a suspension of disbelief. To me, that means a suspension of cynicism, skepticism, and the resignation to the mundane disenchantment of mere existence. To some, a suspension of disbelief might imply a denial of reality and a childish retreat into fantasy. But cartoon characters possess a life in that fourth dimension of human experience called faith.

There is a reality to cartoons that cannot be denied. Cartoons symbolize enchantment, the human heart's instinctive need for laughter, and the magical genius that lives in each of our own imaginations. These qualities are realities. They exist within us all. The universal response of enduring love, nostalgia, and the innocent fascination for animation entertainment is to me a heartwarming affirmation of healthy human possibilities.

Most amazing of all to me is the fundamental spirit of friendship cartoons communicate to those who love them. Looking back over miles and years of countless frames of footage, I can see how that one quality of comradeship runs constant. From Tom and Jerry to Ruff and Reddy, Yogi and Boo Boo, or Fred and Barney, or for that matter, Bill and Joe or Hanna-Barbera and Company, we were always on the buddy system.

Friendship and laughter in the spirit of our cartoons is an exuberant experience which, like many things in the field of animation, often defies description by conventional means. That never stops us in cartoonmaking. When all else fails, we invent.

Several years ago I was asked to explain my own interpretation of the spirit of fellowship and goodwill that Joe and I had always hoped to foster in our work. Well, Joe has always been the one with the silver tongue, and quite honestly I was at a loss for words. After consulting Shakespeare, Bacon, and Mark Twain for a suitable quoted reference, I turned at last to a blustery buddy dressed in animal skins for help.

I don't know if these words merit being chiseled in stone, but here is what we came up with.

YABBA DABBA DOO (yabuh dabuh do͞o) interj.— An expression of jubilance; a spontaneous, loud exclamation of joy; an exchange of greetings between good friends denoting respect and admiration.

Hanna-Barbera Awards

Academy Awards for Short Subjects (Cartoons)[1]
Yankee Doodle Mouse 1943
Mouse Trouble 1944
Quiet Please! 1945
Cat Concerto 1947
The Little Orphan 1948
Two Mouseketeers 1952
Johann Mouse 1953

[1] All Tom and Jerry shorts at MGM

Academy Award Nominations for Short Subjects (Cartoons)
Puss Gets the Boot 1940
The Night Before Christmas 1941
Dr. Jekyll and Mr. Mouse 1947
Hatchup Your Troubles 1949
Jerry's Cousin 1950
Touché Pussy Cat 1954
Good Will to Men 1955
One Droopy Knight 1957

Emmy Awards
The Huckleberry Hound Show 1960—Outstanding Achievement in
    Children's Programming
Jack and the Beanstalk (live action and animation)1966—
    Outstanding Children's Special
The Last of the Curlews 1973—Outstanding Achievement in
    Children's Programming
The Runaways (live action) 1974—Outstanding Informational
    Children's Series
The Gathering (live action) 1978—Outstanding Special
The Smurfs 1982—Outstanding Children's Entertainment Series
The Smurfs 1983—Outstanding Children's Entertainment Series
The Last Halloween 1992—Outstanding Children's Program
Bill Hanna and Joe Barbera 1988—Academy of Television Arts and
    Sciences Governors Award

Annie Award   **Golden Globe Award**
Charlotte's Web 1973   *Hanna-Barbera Presents* 1961

Hollywood Walk of Fame Star
July 21, 1976

Hanna-Barbera Feature Films
Hey There, It's Yogi Bear 1964 Screen Gems
A Man Called Flintstone 1966 Screen Gems
Charlotte's Webb 1973 Paramount
C.H.O.M.P.S. (live action) 1979 American International
Heidi's Song 1982 Paramount

GoBots: Battle of the Rock Lords 1986 Atlantic Releasing
Jetsons: The Movie! 1990 Universal
Tom and Jerry: The Movie 1992
Flintstones 1994 Amblin/Universal

TV Series[2]

Program	First Aired
The Ruff and Reddy Show	1957 NBC
The Huckleberry Hound Show	1958 Syn.
Pixie and Dixie	1958 Syn.
Augie Doggie and Doggie Daddy	1959 Syn.
Quick Draw McGraw	1959 Syn.
Snooper and Blabber	1959 Syn.
Yakky Doodle	1960 Syn.
Hokey Wolf	1960 Syn.
The Flintstones[3]	1960 ABC
Loopy de Loop[4]	1960
Snagglepuss	1960 Syn.
Top Cat	1961 ABC
Lippy the Lion	1962 Syn.
Touché Turtle	1962 Syn.
Wally Gator	1962 Syn.
The Jetsons	1962 ABC
Magilla Gorilla	1963 Syn.
Breezly and Sneezly	1963 Syn.
Yippee, Yappee, and Yahooey	1963 Syn.
Ricochet Rabbit	1963 Syn.
Peter Potamus	1963 Syn.
Punkin Puss	1963 Syn.
Adventures of Jonny Quest	1964 ABC
Secret Squirrel	1965 NBC
Precious Pupp	1965 NBC
The Hillbilly Bears	1965 NBC
Atom Ant	1965 NBC
Winsome Witch	1965 NBC
Squiddly Diddly	1965 NBC

---

[2] Many of these programs for TV metamorphosed over the years, with different titles and slightly different cast arrangements. "Syn." indicates first released in syndication.
[3] The Flintstones family were to appear in many other TV series.
[4] Theatrical cartoons.

Sinbad, Jr.	1965 AIP
Laurel and Hardy	1966 Wolper
Space Kidettes	1966 Syn.
The Space Ghost	1966 CBS
Dino Boy	1966 CBS
Frankenstein, Jr.	1966 CBS
The Impossibles	1966 CBS
Abbott and Costello	1967 RKO-Jomar
Herculoids	1967 CBS
Samson and Goliath	1967 Syn.
The Mighty Mightor	1967 CBS
Moby Dick	1967 CBS
Birdman	1967 NBC
The Fantastic Four	1967 ABC
Shazzan	1967 CBS
The Galaxy Trio	1967 NBC
The Cattanooga Cats	1967 ABC
Banana Splits (live action)	1968 NBC
Danger Island (live action)	1968 NBC
The Three Musketeers	1968 NBC
The Arabian Knights	1968 NBC
The Micro Ventures	1968 NBC
The Adventures of Gulliver	1968 ABC
The New Adventures of Huck Finn (live action)	1968 NBC
The Wacky Races	1968 CBS
The Perils of Penelope Pitstop	1969 CBS
Motormouse and Autocat	1969 ABC
It's the Wolf	1969 ABC
Scooby-Doo, Where Are You?[5]	1969 CBS
Dastardly and Muttley	1969 CBS
Around the World in 79 Days	1969 ABC
The Harlem Globetrotters	1970 CBS
Josie and the Pussycats	1970 CBS
Where's Huddles?	1970 CBS
Pebbles and Bamm Bamm	1971 CBS
Help! It's the Hair Bear Bunch	1971 CBS
The Funky Phantom	1971 ABC
Sealab 2020	1972 NBC
Roman Holidays	1972 NBC

---

[5] The Scooby-Doo gang appeared in many other TV series.

The Amazing Chan and the Chan Clan	1972	CBS
Josie and the Pussycats in Outer Space	1972	CBS
Wait Till Your Father Gets Home	1972	Syn.
Jeannie	1973	CBS
Speed Buggy	1973	CBS
Yogi's Gang	1973	ABC
Peter Puck	1973	ABC
The Addams Family	1973	NBC
Inch High, Private Eye	1973	NBC
Goober and the Ghost Chasers	1973	ABC
Butch Cassidy	1973	NBC
Superfriends[6]	1973	ABC
Honk Kong Phooey	1974	ABC
These Are the Days	1974	ABC
Devlin	1974	ABC
Valley of the Dinosaurs	1974	CBS
Wheelie and the Chopper Bunch	1974	NBC
The Partridge Family: 2200 A.D.	1974	CBS
Korg: 70,000 B.C. (live action)	1974	ABC
The Great Grape Ape	1975	ABC
Tom and Jerry	1975	ABC
Dynomutt	1976	ABC
Jabberjaw	1976	ABC
Mumbly	1976	ABC
Clue Club	1976	CBS
Wonder Wheels	1977	CBS
The C.B. Bears	1977	NBC
Shake, Rattle, and Roll	1977	NBC
Undercover Elephant	1977	NBC
Heyyy, It's the King	1977	NBC
Posse Impossible	1977	NBC
The Robonic Stooges	1977	CBS
Mystery Island (live action)	1977	CBS
Woofer and Wimper, Dog Detectives	1977	CBS
Blast-Off Buzzard	1977	NBC
Captain Caveman and the Teen Angels	1977	ABC
Skatebirds (live action)	1977	CBS
Yogi's Space Race	1978	NBC
The Galaxy Goof-Ups	1978	NBC

---

[6] There were several Superfriends shows over the years.

The Galloping Ghost	1978 NBC
The Buford Files	1978 NBC
Godzilla	1978 NBC
Jana of the Jungle	1978 NBC
The All-New Popeye Hour	1978 CBS
Dinky Dog	1978 CBS
The New Shmoo	1979 NBC
The Super Globetrotters	1979 NBC
Casper and the Angels	1979 NBC
The Thing	1979 NBC
Scooby and Scrappy-Doo	1979 ABC
The Bedrock Cops	1980 NBC
Dino and the Cavemouse	1980 NBC
The Frankenstones	1980 NBC
Captain Caveman	1980 NBC
Drak Pak	1980 CBS
Fonz and the Happy Days Gang	1980 ABC
Richie Rich	1980 ABC
Space Stars	1981 NBC
Astro and the Space Mutts	1981 NBC
Teen Force	1981 NBC
Crazy Claws	1981 CBS
Kwicky Koala	1981 CBS
Dirty Dawg	1981 CBS
The Bungle Brothers	1981 CBS
The Smurfs	1981 NBC
Laverne and Shirley	1981 ABC
Private Olive Oyl	1981 CBS
The Trollkins	1981 CBS
Mork and Mindy	1982 ABC
The Little Rascals	1982 ABC
Pac-Man	1982 ABC
Shirt Tales	1982 NBC
The Gary Coleman Show	1982 NBC
The Dukes	1983 CBS
Monchhichis	1983 ABC
The Biskitts	1983 CBS
Benji (live action)	1983 CBS
Going Bananas (live action)	1984 NBC
The Snorks	1984 NBC
The Pink Panther and Sons	1984 NBC

Challenge of the GoBots	1984	ABC
The Funtastic World of Hanna-Barbera	1985	Syn.
Wildfire	1986	CBS
Pound Puppies	1986	ABC
The Flintstone Kids	1986	ABC
Foofur	1986	NBC
The Flintstone Kids	1987	ABC
Popeye and Son	1987	CBS
Foofur	1987	NBC
The New Yogi Bear Show	1988	Syn.
The Completely Mental Misadventures of Ed Grimley	1988	NBC
Fantastic Max	1988	Syn.
The Adventures of Don Coyote	1989	Syn.
Droopy, with Spike and Tyke	1989	Syn.
Rick Moranis in Gravedale High	1990	NBC
Bill and Ted's Excellent Adventures	1990	CBS
Tom and Jerry Kids	1990	Syn.
The Pirates of Dark Water	1990	Fox
Fender Bender	1990	Syn.
Monster Tails	1990	Syn.
Fish Police	1991	CBS
Young Robin Hood	1991	Syn.
Capitol Critters	1992	ABC
Captain Planet	1992	TBS
Droopy, Master Detective	1993	Syn.
Screwball Squirrel	1993	Syn.
Swat Kats	1993	Syn.
Two Stupid Dogs	1993	TBS
What a Cartoon!	1995	Cartoon Network
The Real Adventures of Jonny Quest	1996	Turner Networks

TV Specials

Special	First Aired	
Alice in Wonderland	1966	ABC
Jack and the Beanstalk	1966	NBC

The Thanksgiving That Almost Wasn't	1971	Syn.
Love American Style (*Wait Till Your Father Gets Home* pilot)	1971	Syn.
Love and the Private Eye, Melvin Danger	1971	
A Christmas Story	1971	Syn.
Last of the Curlews	1972	
Yogi's Ark Lark	1972	ABC
Oliver and the Artful Dodger	1972	ABC
Here Come the Clowns	1972	ABC
Gidget Makes the Wrong Connection	1972	ABC
The Banana Splits in Hocus-Pocus Park	1972	ABC
20,000 Leagues under the Sea	1973	Syn.
The Three Musketeers	1973	Syn.
Lost in Space	1973	ABC
The Count of Monte Cristo	1973	Syn.
The Runaways	1974	ABC
Crazy Comedy Concert (live action and animated)	1974	ABC
The Last of the Mohicans	1975	
Phantom Rebel (live action)	1976	NBC
Davy Crockett on the Mississippi	1976	CBS
Taggart's Treasure (live action pilot)	1976	ABC
Five Weeks in a Balloon	1977	CBS
Yabba-Dabba-Doo! The World of Hanna-Barbera (live action and animated)	1977	CBS
The Flintstones' Christmas	1977	NBC
Energy: A National Issue	1977	Syn.
Beach Girls (live action pilot)	1977	Syn.
It Isn't Easy Being a Teenage Millionaire (live action)	1978	ABC
Hanna-Barbera's Happy Hour	1978	NBC
Hanna-Barbera's All-Star Comedy Ice Review (live action and animated)	1978	CBS
Cyrano de Bergerac	1974	ABC
The Flintstones' Little Big League	1978	NBC
Black Beauty	1978	CBS
The Funny World of Fred and Bunni (live action and animated)	1978	CBS
Yabba-Dabba-Doo II	1979	CBS
Superheroes Roast (live action)	1979	NBC
Challenge of the Superheroes (live action)	1979	NBC
America vs. the World Circus Challenge (live)	1979	NBC

Scooby Goes Hollywood	1979	ABC
Casper's First Christmas	1979	NBC
Sgt. T.K. Yu (live action pilot)	1979	NBC
Popeye: Sweethearts at Sea	1979	CBS
Gulliver's Travels	1979	CBS
Casper's Halloween Special: He Ain't Scary, He's Our Brother	1979	NBC
The Flintstones' New Neighbors	1980	NBC
Fred's Final Fling	1980	NBC
Yogi's First Christmas	1980	OPT
The Flintstones Meet Rockula and Frankenstone	1980	NBC
B.B. Beegle (puppets)	1980	Syn.
The Hanna-Barbera Arena Show (live)	1981	NBC
Jogging Fever	1981	NBC
Wind-Up Wilma	1981	NBC
The Great Gilly Hopkins (live action)	1981	CBS
Daniel Boone	1981	CBS
The Smurfs	1981	NBC
The Smurfs' Springtime Special	1982	NBC
The Jokebook	1982	NBC
The Smurfs' Christmas Special	1982	NBC
Christmas Comes to Pac-Land	1982	ABC
Yogi Bear's All-Star Christmas Caper	1982	CBS
My Smurfy Valentine	1983	NBC
The Smurfic Games	1984	NBC
Smurfily Ever After	1985	NBC
Star Fairies	1985	Syn.
Pound Puppies	1985	Syn.
The Flintstones' 25th Anniversary Celebration	1986	CBS
'Tis the Season To Be Smurfy	1987	NBC
Yellow Bus (live action pilot)		
The Little Troll Prince	1987	Syn.
The Flintstone Kids: "Just Say No"	1988	ABC
Hanna-Barbera's 50th: A Yabba-Dabba-Doo Celebration (live action and animated)	1989	TNT
Hagar and the Horrible	1989	CBS
I Yabba Dabba Do!	1992	ABC
Flintstones Family Christmas	1993	ABC
Halloween Tree	1993	TBS
Hollyrock-a-Bye Baby	1993	ABC
Arabian Nights	1994	TBS

Best of Bedrock	1994	Fox
Daisy Head Maizie	1994	TNT
A Flintstone Christmas Carol	1994	TBS
Yogi the Easter Bear	1994	TBS
Jonny Quest vs. the Cyber Insects	1995	TNT

TV Features

Feature	Year Aired	
Hardcase (live action)	1972	ABC
Shootout in a One Dog Town (live action)	1974	ABC
The Gathering (live action)	1977	ABC
The Beasts Are in the Streets (live action)	1978	NBC
KISS Meets the Phantom of the Park (live action)	1978	NBC
The Gathering, Part II (live action)	1979	NBC
Belle Starr (live action)	1980	CBS
The Gymnast (live action)	1980	ABC
Lucky Luke	1985	Syn.
The Stone Fox	1987	NBC
UltraMan	1987	Syn.
The Hanna-Barbera Superstars: Ten Movies	1987–1989	Syn.

      Yogi and the Magical Flight of the Spruce Goose
      The Good, the Bad, and Huckleberry Hound
      Yogi's Great Escape
      The Jetsons Meet the Flintstones
      Top Cat and the Beverly Hills Cats
      Scooby-Doo Meets the Boo Brothers
      Scooby-Doo and the Ghoul School
      Yogi and the Invasion of the Space Bears
      Scooby-Doo and the Reluctant Werewolf
      Rockin' with Judy Jetson

Rock Odyssey	1989 International
The Dreamer of Oz	1991
The Last Halloween	1992

Home Video

The Greatest Adventure: Stories from the Bible	1986–1990

      "The Creation"
      "The Nativity"

"Moses"
"Daniel and the Lion's Den"
"Noah's Ark"
"David and Goliath"
"Sampson and Delilah"
"Joshua and the Battle of Jerico"
"Joseph and His Brothers"
"The Easter Story"

This acclaimed video series for children has won two Gold Angel awards from Religion in Media, two Awards of Excellence from the Film Advisory Board, and a Distinguished Service Award and Golden Eagle Award from National Religious Broadcasters.
Timeless Tales   1989–1991

Index

Note: Page numbers in *italics* indicate illustrations.